Contents

Introduction

Children are an essential part of everyone's life. They are innocent and fragile. Whether we have children or not, we know we must protect them. But what should we protect them from?

Today, the government has increased its intense demands on children. It is believed that children do not belong to their parents; that, in fact, their parents have no rights over them. An excellent example is Norway, where the state agency for child protection removes children from their families without serious arguments. The system in Norway has reached an absurd situation - children are taken away against their will, resulting in mental trauma in them, not to speak of their parents.

But that is not all. It is believed that children should be raised and educated systematically by various institutions - schools, NGOs, and government agencies. Parents only have to follow the already set requirements without having the right to their own vote. Parents today have almost no say when it comes to worldview education - the liberal worldview completely dominates legislation in most schools and universities, not to mention the media. Even if a parent does not want their child to learn about evolution, the so-called LGBT communities, and supposed global warming, they have no choice.

In this way, the liberal worldview is easily imposed on children who are expected to be tolerant of LGBT communities. The idea of "gender reassignment" in children is encouraged, as well as "sex/sexual education" from an early age. Books are published to "educate" children in a new way so that they readily accept this liberal worldview.

The result of all this is that children become increasingly confused about their moral values. They have an unstable worldview that quickly changes according to their experiences. They distrust their parents and friends; they start believing in the theory of individualism. It is even more frightening when children are encouraged to change their gender or undergo sexual experiments. It is not only about morality; the mental health of our children is and will be damaged.

Now we turn to the subject and content of this work. It contains five chapters. The first one is engaged with one vital issue: to whom do children belong? Here we will consider the problem of the relationship between parents, children, and the government. Who exactly do children "belong" to? Who has more rights over them - the parents or the government? When does the government have the right to remove children from their families? Here we will present some shocking examples from Norway showing that the government should not exceed its powers. Children are first of all brought up by their parents, and it should not be so easy to put them in institutions. We will also refer to Plato, who claims that the government should raise and educate children. This conception will be shown to be immoral and unjustifiable.

The second chapter deals with sex/sexual education. The position that children's education should be centrally planned and parents should only follow this planning is clearly seen in the practice of sex education. This is an education that supposedly focuses on human biology, but, in fact, it is mainly concerned with the propaganda of the so-called LGBT communities and imposed tolerance towards these people. Projects to conduct sex education in kindergartens in some European countries are outrageous-typical examples are Germany and Sweden. We will show that children cannot be subjected to such an experiment because they possess a fragile psyche. Sex education as we see it today will only lead to more early pregnancies and mass fornication. This type of education should be banned below the age of 13 (when children are already entering their teenage years).

The third chapter is focused on homeschooling as an alternative way to educate our children. One of the options for opposing this violent imposition of the liberal worldview is precisely homeschooling. Here we will look at what are the advantages and disadvantages of this education. Homeschooling is a good option for parents who do not trust educational institutions. However, these parents must be well prepared in advance and undergo special training while their children are still young. We must note that this education shows some shortcomings.

Another chapter concerns patriotic education. Children today learn to be tolerant of all the cultures that are present in the life of this country. That is wonderful, but where is patriotism, or love of Fatherland? These children will be cut off from their family environment, from their roots. It is time for patriotic education to return to school as it was during the Cold War.

Here we should also mention the need for more vital religious education in school. Let those children who want to learn about the God of Christians do it. This should be entirely of their own free will and without causing harm to other children. America is a Christian country and that should not be forgotten; history cannot be changed.

The problem of the media is the subject of the last chapter. Today, the media enjoys almost complete freedom to spread whatever it wants. Where is its responsibility for what it shows? What is its impact on children? How do violence and erotic elements affect children's minds? We will analyze these issues. We will prove that stricter control of the media is necessary from the point of view of proper upbringing. Movies with excessive violence or eroticism should not be allowed on television or in movie theaters at all. It is high time we ended this radicalization of the media and made it clear where the red line is.

Of course, we already know all this. What can be done about these issues? Can we protect our children from this moral decay? Yes, it is quite possible, and we should not give up fighting for our worldview. Because true tolerance is precisely this - that each person can safely raise their children in what they believe in, without harming others. The Christian worldview does not harm society but actually makes it stable and confident.

Much more is to be said regarding the difficult times we are facing today. The present work focuses only on some topics such as education and upbringing. We can go even further and discuss morality, art, science, and even modern ways of entertainment. We have chosen to deal with the topic of education due to our belief that education is the key to the creation of good and responsible citizens and human beings. The book is thus devoted to the relations between parents, children and government. There are, of course, other factors influencing these relations: friends, job, entertainment activities, economy, political activity, etc. It is beyond the scope of this work to engage with such subjects.

And finally, some words about methodology. This book will deal primarily with moral issues, but it will also analyze educational, legislative, and policy issues. We will combine philosophy with theology, ethics, and psychology. If we are to counter this disastrous influence the media and contemporary curriculum have on our children, we need to respond in all possible spheres of human activity.

The Christian worldview will be only partially discussed here, but the reader should bear in mind the suggestion that it is only this worldview that could ensure the stability and political health of our society, of America as a whole.

Chapter I: To whom do children "belong"?

Children are human beings, no doubt about it. However, the fact is that they used to be disenfranchised for a very long time. Children used to be exploited as workers; they were not protected in any way. In fact, they used to be treated like adults, even though children were not well developed either physically or mentally. They performed the duties of adults but did not enjoy not their rights. It was only in the 20th century that children began to be considered equal citizens. All of this happened alongside the women's rights movement and the view that all people are equal before the law, regardless of their gender, ethnicity, or social background.

In the past, children were entirely under the care of their families. Their parents or siblings were responsible for them. Very rarely did the state or state institutions intervene.

However, various agencies and other institutions for the protection of children emerged over time. They are based on the principle that children sometimes need external protection, i.e., by agents who are not biased and can assess their situation objectively. There are cases in which these agencies must intervene: physical violence; labor exploitation of children (which became prohibited only at the beginning of the 20th century); sexual abuse. Undoubtedly, there are many different reasons for the intervention of external forces that aim to preserve the health and normal life of children.

Our book deals with the problem of how to protect children. Here we will examine two opposing conceptions that address this problem:

(1) the conception of complete family autonomy- the family should have freedom regarding all aspects of education and upbringing. The government can intervene only in extreme cases. Parental rights are absolutely granted.

(2) the conception of government (external) intervention- children "belong" to the government, to the authorities. Their parents should be controlled and monitored by governmental or state agencies. Parental rights are restricted to protect children.

To compare both of them, we will first begin with the second conception, which is exemplified in the doctrine expressed in Plato's *Republic*.

1.1 Plato's doctrine of "shared children"

Summary:

Plato first expressed the position that children could be raised by a special group of people. He suggests this so that they can be loyal to the state alone, while blood ties can only tear them away from the idea of the good of the state as a whole.

Plato is the first philosopher in whom we see a clearly expressed conception of children's upbringing. Yes, we all associate Plato with idealism. We know him as a pagan whose ideas came near Christianity. He proved logically that God exists and that the soul is immortal. Plato also posed the problem of goodness and justice very often.

But, like any other philosopher, Plato had his weaknesses. His doctrine of the state was created during a period of tragic wars that broke out in Ancient Greece. Athens, the cradle of democracy, lost the war against undemocratic Sparta. Well-prepared militarily, Sparta put an end to Athens' ambitions to spread its model of government to other Greek polises (city-states). Plato made the logical (albeit incorrect) conclusion that democracy leads to lost wars. That is why he created a conception of the state and society, which today seems to us highly totalitarian.

Of course, Plato's book itself focuses on several themes: goodness, justice, philosophy. Thus the problem of the treatment of children can only be interpreted in this context. Plato understands the ideal state as the embodiment of goodness; according to him, it should be organized in such a way as to meet the criteria of a good and just state.

In conducting his analysis, Plato employs the method of maieutics. This is a special type of dialogue where questions are asked without waiting for certain answers. The aim of maieutics is to arrive at the truth gradually as if it were "born." Thus, the reader is left with the impression that Socrates is indeed leading his interlocutors to the truth. But in fact, Socrates knows this truth in advance and uses all sorts of sophist methods to confuse his interlocutors (and opponents).

Speaking of proper upbringing, Socrates (actually Plato) argued that young people should not think that the gods have sins and vices. The gods are supposed to be role models, but instead, the Greek poets portray them as having typical human frailties. As Socrates states, "Stories about Hera being chained by her son, on the other hand, or about Hephaestus being hurled from heaven by his father when he tried to save his mother from a beating... should not be admitted into our city, either as allegories or nonallegories." Proper education demands that such narratives be banned because they make young people think that it is normal to be bad and unjust. As Socrates explains, "the beliefs they absorb at that age are difficult to erase and tend to become unalterable. For these reasons, then, we should probably take the utmost care to ensure that the first stories they hear about virtue are the best ones for them to hear" (Republic 377e).

Plato is absolutely right here: it is very important what we teach our children while they are young. If we tell them that their role models are actually bad people, then there is nothing else we can expect from these kids than to do the same as those role models. If gods commit sins, then children will perceive these acts as acceptable.

Therefore, what should be done? According to Socrates (Plato), such stories should be forbidden in the ideal city, and poets should be strictly controlled: "We will compel the poets either to deny that they did such things, or else to deny that they were children of the gods. But they must not say both or attempt to persuade our young people that the gods produce evils, nor that heroes are no better than humans." Here Plato adds that "After all, as we were saying earlier, these things are neither pious nor true" (Republic 391e).

In short, we must be careful what the content of the teaching material is; it does not matter what is true and what is not true - the only important thing is what effect this information will have on the upbringing of the children! If any information makes children think that it is okay to be unfair and immoral, then it should be eliminated immediately. Whether we want it or not, the information we offer our children must pass through a certain filter, through censorship - and this is quite natural.

But now we come to that part of Plato's conception that seems quite unrealistic. This is the assumption that people should be divided into classes according to the type of work they do - for example, guards or craftsmen (or people who produce something).

According to Plato, *we should abolish the family* as a social unit and raise our children together with other people. Here is what it all looks like:

Plato first begins with the idea that only the whole is better than the partial, the individual. It would be best for us to live together without having much wealth or property of our own. It will make us better citizens. But beyond that, marriage must be abolished. Any woman can have relationships with any man over a certain age! Here we see the purpose of this elimination of marriage: "All these women should be shared among all the men, that no individual woman and man should live together, and that the children, too, should be shared, with no parent knowing its own offspring, and no child its parent" (Republic 457d).

Yes, this is what Plato wants in his ideal state - *no special relationship between parents and children*! Children should belong to the state (although he does not quite put it that way). They should not have knowledge regarding who their parents are; they should not be bound in any way to specific people.

But Plato goes even further. He directly talks about eugenics. Let us take the best men and women and match them, he writes: "The best men should mate with the best women in as many cases as possible, while the opposite should hold of the worst men and women; and that the offspring of the former should be reared, but not that of the latter, if our flock is going to be an eminent one" (Republic 459e). He adds that only rulers or the ruling elite can access this information. In a word, the state carries out a policy of eugenics in the hope that "better children" will be born this way. They will be wholly devoted to the state (that is, to their rulers) and will have no personal claim to anything. They will be raised in a special way so that they cannot find their biological parents. We do not even mention here that the "worse children" will simply disappear, that is, they will be killed - something that was practiced in Sparta then.

But how can we raise children without their birth parents being involved? We need to create a unique profession - female nannies to take care of these children from a young age. These women will be something like their mothers, though not exactly. The children will be gathered together and live with the nannies in question, without any mention of family or kinship relationships. As the Greek philosopher writes, the rulers "will take the offspring of good parents to the rearing pen and hand them over to special nurses who live in a separate part of the city. But those of inferior parents, or any deformed offspring of the others, they will hide in a secret and unknown place" (Republic 460c).

Yet, things seem more complicated now. In another place, Plato speaks of mothers. He asks the following question: "And won't these nurses also take care of the children's feeding by bringing the mothers to the rearing pen when their breasts are full...? And won't they provide other women as wet nurses if the mothers themselves have insufficient milk" (Republic 460d).

After all the children live together, how can we even talk about mothers? The core of this doctrine is that children do not live with their biological mothers. Here Plato gets a little confused. However, he adds that women can be mothers as long as they bear children. But - attention - not all women should have this right! Women between 20-40 can raise children, and men between 30-55 will be *allowed* to beget children (Republic 460e). All other ages are inappropriate, and such men and women should not be allowed to have intimate relations. If a woman over 40 mates with a man over 55, their child will probably have some kind of disability - this is the logic followed by Plato. And there is something true in that, but the fact is that there is no way the law prohibits intimate relations for people over a certain age.

It is logical to ask - well, if someone does violate this prohibition, what will happen to the children who will be born in this "criminal way"? Plato does not mention anything about abortion, although, at that time, the concept of abortion already existed. But he has in mind something far more cruel - such children will simply be killed after birth so as not to risk "degrading the quality" of the citizens of the ideal state.

Rearing children by a particular group of women is not Plato's only suggestion regarding the family in the ideal city-state. He adds that it is essential that citizens have access to both pain and pleasure. In war, they exist together and form one whole. However, the same can be said about pleasure - the abolition of marriage will allow them to have more sources of pleasure, and thus, they will be satisfied with the order and organization of the ideal state. As Plato states, "Well, doesn't sharing pleasure and pain bind it together—when, as far as possible, all the citizens feel more or less the same joy or pain at the same gains or losses?" (Plato 462b)

Plato's conception must be analyzed in the context of the wars that Athens fought with Sparta, as well as the fact that at that time, the idea of monogamy was not as strong as it is today. Without a doubt, monogamy, as we know it today, appeared with Christianity. Paganism allowed promiscuous intimate relationships, and in Ancient Greece, homosexuality was accepted by society. Therefore, even 2,500 years ago, this concept does not seem shocking. However, what may surprise people of all times and countries is the idea of joint child rearing. Since the beginning of human history, people have raised their children in smaller or larger families; however, children were never perceived as "common." Even today, we can see exactly this: the most backward tribes in Brazil or in Oceania do not adhere to such a practice. The parental instinct is very strong, and no sane parent would give their child to other people to raise except in exceptional circumstances.

The errors of Platon's conception are not few. Among them, we can mention the following shortcomings:

1. The view that the general should dominate the individual is wrong. A given society must also take care of the individual needs of its members.

2. The idea of "sharing" women is completely immoral. This degrades us to the level of animals whose sole purpose is to mate to produce offspring. Plato offers the possibility for the "nobler" men to have relations with any woman they want. This is mere debauchery, not a philosophical doctrine.

3. Raising children by other people rather than their biological parents removes the parental instinct. What motivation will these professional women have to raise other people's children? What will be the criteria of this cultivation? Who will control them? How exactly will these women be selected?

4. What will happen to the inheritance relationship between parents and children? Yes, Plato mentions that records of these relationships must be kept somewhere. But the idea of the common upbringing of children completely negates the principle of inheritance. Many children could claim to be the heirs of some distinguished citizen of the ideal state.

All this shows that Plato's ideal state is not at all the realization and embodiment of goodness. This is simply his personal vision of a social system that is no different from a dictatorship. The difference with other similar conceptions is that here the philosophers rule the state.

All these weaknesses aside, we see something essential here: the view that children belong to the state (that is, the government) and not to their biological (or foster) parents. According to Plato, children should be used as a tool to strengthen and stabilize the state. These are children brought up in love and loyalty to their country. They are raised through myths to teach them such loyalty. They should think only good things about their country and, of course, their rulers.

Today, however, the understanding of children's belonging to the state is based on another principle- namely, that children are endowed with absolute rights and no one has the right to limit them. Proponents of the second conception mentioned earlier believe that the family only reduces these rights, therefore control should be shifted from the family (parents) to the state. Hence, we will now turn our attention to specific examples that show the fallacy of this conception.

1.2 The Scandinavian system for removal of children from their families

Summary:

Here we look specifically at Norway's "child protection" system, or Barnevernet. We will discuss several controversial cases of removed children and reflect on what is the cause of it. We will show how harmful is the conception that children "belong" to the state.

Here we will talk about a system that does not officially exist under the name "Scandinavian." The Scandinavian "child protection" system is characterized by common features of the systems existing in Sweden, Norway, and Denmark. Norway stands out among these systems with numerous cases of child removal from their families, so we will deal more with this European country.

Before starting our analysis, we need to explain the social and political context of the "child protection" system in Nordic countries. The Scandinavian nations expose a strong collective mentality, which means that the individual is strongly oppressed and must follow the rules imposed by the collective. Individualism has almost no place in these societies. Rules are defined to favor the good of the societies themselves, not the individuals within them.

Quite logically, there is a strong bias towards socialism in the Scandinavian countries. Yes, this is not communism in its Stalinist version, but still countries like Sweden and Norway have been ruled by socialists for decades. Of course, sometimes conservatives take power there. But in general, even conservatives are forced to be "more leftist" because that is the only way they can win more votes.

In view of all that has been said, it is not surprising that in both Sweden and Norway, the conception of the equality of all people has been raised into a cult. It is no coincidence that radical feminism and LGBT ideology have a strong presence there. At the political level, it is scarce to express any criticism of these ideologies and concepts.

The topic of the absolute emancipation of women there is like a dogma - not subject to discussion or criticism. At the same time, citizens are forced to believe that only the state has the right to control their children. From a young age, Swedes and Norwegians are taught that state institutions protect them and their parents can go to jail in case of any violence.

Undoubtedly, we are talking about mentality and culture here. Norwegian and Swedish citizens agree to the state removing their children if any rules are broken. Unlike the United States, citizens there prefer to accept such a decision and very rarely resist. Civil resistance is almost unknown in the Scandinavian countries.

Nonetheless, all this does not mean that Norway and Sweden are dictatorships. This would not be a good definition. Rather, they are an example of another approach to human rights and the state-citizen relationship. This is an approach where removing children from their parents is considered right, whereas in America, it is seen as violence (at least in most cases).

We begin our research with an open letter to the ECHR[1] in Strasbourg from the Nordic Committee for Human Rights for the Protection of Family Rights in Nordic Countries. As we said, Scandinavian citizens rarely protest against the authorities' decisions, but still, there are organizations for the protection of parents in these countries as well. In this 2012 letter, parental rights advocates shed light on various cases of forced and unjustified child removal. According to them, the criteria for withdrawal are often based on discrimination. As the letter says, "it appears that mostly young, single parent families, economically and educationally weaker families, families with health challenges

---

[1] European Court of Human Rights- a Court that deals with issues related to fundamental human rights across Europe.

and immigrant parents are targeted by the social services in Sweden, Norway, Denmark and Finland." So it turns out that for a poor immigrant parent, the chances of keeping their child if they are investigated by the social services are very slim. But in addition, "parents with religious and philosophical beliefs, which do not seem to be politically accepted, are often deemed as unsuitable parents" (NCHR 1).

As we see here, the problem is not simply what the relationship between parents and children is, but that the state decides to analyze and monitor the behavior of parents. Are these parents "capable"? Can they take care of their children "properly"? In fact, these are the questions that an organization like Barnevernet - or the child "protection" service in Norway - deals with.

According to this committee, the Norwegian and Swedish legislation went too far without any justification. Social workers are given too much freedom to decide individual cases. As the people from the committee write, "The law was made to protect children who are in danger, but very often it is used arbitrarily, by the social workers and by the administrative courts, where no legal grounds to remove a child are obvious" (NCHR 4).

The main principle followed by the social workers in question is to remove children from "problem parents" as quickly as possible. However, the question is how they identify these "problem parents." In most cases, it turns out that these are not people who abuse alcohol or drugs; nor parents who beat their children. Moreover, the citizens of Norway and Sweden know very well what the systematic use of alcohol can lead to there - taking away their children is absolutely certain in such a case, even if the other parent does not consume alcohol at all. As we have said, the principle is that children should be taken as quickly as possible from the family itself; it does not matter which parent is to blame, it does not matter if the children have close relatives - they should be immediately taken away and sent to a "safe place" that remains anonymous for a long time!

This principle is harmful to the children themselves. In fact, social services around the world are generally guided by the principle that the child should be left with close relatives and not completely isolated from them. Why should a child not be able to stay with their grandparents, or uncle and aunt? The child already knows them well, and they know the child; they know what the needs and interests of a given child are. As it is pointed out in the Letter of NCHR, "The transfer of custody of the foster children from their parents cuts all ties between the children and their parents, and the parents lose all say in the lives of their children" (NCHR 7). Relationships between children and their loved ones must be preserved. But why do not social services in Norway and Sweden do this?

The authors of the letter refer to a study of the cases of children taken in Sweden between 1920 and 1990. It turns out that quite a few of the children suffered from hunger and did not receive health care. Of course, most tragic cases are from a few decades ago, but even today, such accidents can happen. Therefore, the authors state that "The children were removed from conditions that the authorities deemed to be unfavorable, but instead of receiving better living conditions, they had been brutalised, harassed, insulted, mentally, physically and even sexually abused" (NCHR 9-10). Why, then, should an investigation take place several decades after a case? Why is there no transparency and normal access to information? Why are parents viewed as potential criminals?

To all this, we can add another important question: who cares about the children's opinion? What do they want, what do they need? This apparently does not matter much to social services. This is exactly what the authors from the NCHR conclude: "It is an established fact that, in Swedish social work child protection investigations and child custody investigations there is scarce or no information received from the child" (NCHR 14). The kids are just transferred from one place to another, and that is it. They are not told much and are forbidden to keep in touch with their parents. This isolation violates the rights of both children and their parents. The social services in the Scandinavian countries usurp the functions of the state and arbitrarily take and hide children without normal access to this information. That is why the authors of this letter seek support from the Court in Strasbourg and the Council of Europe. They want to file lawsuits against the countries violating the rights of the parents and the children themselves: "It is indeed high time that the organs of the Council of Europe should investigate the violations of children's and their parents' Human Rights that are being perpetrated by the social authorities and the administrative court systems" (NCHR 16).

The truth is that a parent would have a hard time winning a court case in Strasbourg against state institutions because they are relying on national legislation. R The Strasbourg court can rather determine whether legislation contains contradictions and whether a legal act of a state institution violates a human right. The problem is with the legislation itself. It is not natural for a state agency to interpret the interests of the child on its own, without ever consulting the child or his close people.

From this letter, we learn many more facts that we are not going to analyze now. There are also some outrageous cases of children removed without any serious reason.

The Scandinavian system of "child care" shows the weaknesses of the centralized approach. With it, children are taken away without clear grounds, as well as according to discriminatory criteria. The children of immigrants, as well as of parents in a more difficult economic situation, are often taken away. Common sense tells us that it should be the other way around - unemployed people should be supported rather than subjected to institutional abuse. A child feels good in his environment, and any attempt to forcibly change that environment will only create trauma in the child.

In an article from 2018, two other defenders of parents' rights, Simonsen and Haslev Skånland, describe a case that shows there is something wrong with Barnevernet's system. It is about an expert at Barnevernet, a person with enormous experience and authority, who turns out to be a pedophile. As these authors write, "A child psychiatrist and top child protection expert, 56-year-old Jo Erik Brøyn, who in 2010 became the single father to two Indian surrogate babies, has been sentenced to nearly two years' jail under Norway's child pornography laws" (Simonsen, Haslev Skånland par. 1). He was possessing and sharing videos and photos of sexual abuse of children, and also adopted two Indian babies. It is only logical to assume that this person will go to prison and will no longer be allowed any access to children. But things appear to be shocking for the neutral reader. It turns out that the Barnevernet hold themselves to a double standard, i.e., they break their own rules. Here is how:

The pedophile in question receives very delicate treatment. He is allowed to communicate with his adopted children, and his sister is also allowed to care for them - something contrary to Barnevernet's practice (though allowed by that organization's rules). As these authors observe, "When Brøyn was arrested more than a year ago, his children were at first allowed to be placed with his sister... Before Brøyn was released from custody, his children were moved by the CPS to non-relatives."

However, he is subsequently allowed to reunite with his children - something that has no reasonable explanation at all. In other cases, where the parents have no fault, the children are simply taken away (in most cases, in secret). According to Simonsen and Haslev Skånland, this is a manifestation of a double standard: "The liberal attitude of a section of the authorities, here regarding a confessed pedophile father living alone with his children, is somewhat unusual. In open court Brøyn stated that he has pedophile leanings, being stimulated by sexual pictures and films of boys" (Simonsen, Haslev Skånland par. 6). Is there not something else hidden behind this - for example, an attempt to cover up the case and stop public discontent? And how is it even possible to give a pedophile access to his children? Does Norwegian law allow this?

But that is not all. Brøyn himself violates his professional principles and practice. He is described as a person that always recommends that the child be separated forever from his parents and relatives. However, here he is eager to have the opposite - his relatives to take care of the children. As the authors note, "Our thoughts go to the thousands of cases in which the CPS and their psychologists have insisted not only on depriving children of their biological parents, but have rejected out of hand entirely capable carers such as grandparents, uncles and aunts, grown-up siblings" (Simonsen, Haslev Skånland par. 8). In short, people who are part of Barnevernet enjoy enormous privileges. Suddenly it turns out that it is possible for a child to be placed with an uncle and aunt, with grandparents; but in most cases, this does not happen. Why is that?

But there are other questions to be asked here. How come the people around this pedophile, the other experts, didn't notice what was going on? It is not possible for a pedophile to hide himself so well that no one knows this. Quite reasonably, Simonsen and Haslev Skånland ask: "Have no experts in the CEC or other colleagues been aware that Brøyn has kept up nefarious activities relating to children for 20 years? He has in several periods been going to therapy himself, relating to his problems with sexuality and his pedophile leanings" (Simonsen, Haslev Skånland par. 21).

We can only conclude that this man is part of a larger network and that there is special protection over him. There is no other way to explain the fact that he was sentenced to only one year and ten months in prison! It is true that the Norwegian justice system is very soft on criminals, but this is a real absurdity. What is this system that takes away a child because a parent is not paid well, and at the same time, sends a proven pedophile to prison for less than two years? It is clear that the system itself is flawed, and this case is not a huge exception.

This is exactly what the authors want to demonstrate - Barnevernet acts differently in similar cases, and this is due to the bias of the individuals involved. Instead of following the same rules and practices, these individuals decide for themselves when and how to remove a child. This case, the authors note, "stands in some contrast to the propaganda overflowing in Norway from those quarters in our media daily, urging especially people in public employ to report to the CPS any suspicion, however vague, of something worrying concerning the care of children" (Simonsen, Haslev Skånland par. 25).

Norwegian social services are said to have already launched an investigation into previous cases involving the pedophile in question. So far, however, there are no official data on what exactly happened to the children taken from their parents at his discretion. It can be assumed that Brøyn had a vested interest in some way, but this has so far not been proven. It would not be surprising if more cases like this popped up and it turns out that there are more pedophiles working throughout the Barnevernet system, pedophiles that kidnap children and then send them to people who sexually abuse them.

Following this shocking report, we continue our analysis with two extreme cases of child abduction in Norway. In a 2016 article for the BBC, Tim Whewell exposes a few cases where children were taken without any justification.

The first case describes the tragedy of Marius (Romanian) and Ruth (Norwegian). Their four children were taken suddenly on a day in 2015 by people in two cars; no explanation was given. The next day another car even took their baby! The parents were arrested and interrogated like real criminals.

The reason for the removal turned out to be information from the principal of the school, where two daughters study, that the parents were hitting their children. In casual conversation, children said this without realizing what the consequences might be. Their words were taken as absolutely true without any attempt at investigation. Parents admitted that they sometimes slap their children, but not in a systematic way and without causing trauma, which can easily be diagnosed by a doctor. Children were then simply taken away without medical examination, without sufficient evidence of physical abuse. Therefore, it is logical to assume that the reason is different. The parents turned out to be very religious people, and it is possible that this is the real reason for the children being removed from them. Although being religious is not forbidden in Norway, social services there believe that children have the right to form their own worldview. But how can this happen without the involvement of parents?

This tragic case led to massive protests by human rights organizations and other organizations around the world. As Whewell notes, "Thousands of people have joined demonstrations in support of Ruth and Marius in a series of countries across four continents. The Norwegian child protection service... has been accused by protesters of 'kidnapping' children - in this and many other cases" (Whewell par. 10).

As Whewell reports, the main issue here is that "it's impossible to find out the authorities' side of the story, because the child protection service won't discuss individual cases, to protect children's privacy" (Whewell par. 17). Everything takes place in complete mystery, without informing the parents. Marius is forbidden to even speak his native language to the children! After all, for the next seven months, "the children were split between three different sets of emergency foster parents. Marius and Ruth had an eight-hour round trip to get to supervised meetings with the baby, and separately with the two older boys" (Whewell par. 19). Children were not just taken away, but separated from each other - something that is hard to imagine. During this time, their anxiety increased – would they ever see their parents, brothers, sisters? Will they ever enter their native home?

The case was so absurd that public pressure forced Barnevernet to change its mind. Seven months after the initial removal, the children were returned to their parents. Marius and Ruth, of course, decided to leave Norway, even though it meant huge financial and emotional losses for them. A case before the court in Strasbourg followed, which, however, was terminated in 2020. The family never received compensation for its unjustified separation and the mental trauma caused.

It is good that this trial ended fairly. But there are similar cases, and they do not end well at all. Of course, they usually happen with one or two children. Taking away five children is a terrible thing, and it is difficult for the system to cope with mass protests. But taking a child away is easy and quiet.

The Barnevernet justifies its actions by saying that taking away children is only done as a last resort. But the truth is that these people do it very quickly, regardless of whether there is enough evidence. The court then determines whether Barnevernet's decision was correct; but what happens to the children during this time? They are sent to foster families, to a foreign environment, and sometimes they do not even know the language (if they are from an immigrant family). Whewell remarks that "The child protection service, Barnevernet, stresses that in the vast majority of cases when it thinks something's going wrong in a family, it doesn't take the children away. It works with parents to solve the problems and keep the family together" (Whewell par. 31).

But the next case we will discuss shows the opposite. A child can be taken away based on the subjective judgment of social workers: "Most cases now don't involve parental violence, though, or alcohol- or drug-abuse. The commonest reason for a care order now is simply 'lack of parenting skills'" (Whewell par. 33). As this journalist notes, "That, in short, is the reason Barnevernet gave for taking away the four-month-old baby daughter of a young Norwegian father called Erik and his Chinese wife in the country's second city, Bergen" (Whewell par. 34). The reason for the removal was that very often the child's grandmother took care of the child, which is an unusual practice in Norway.

Social services assumed the mother had some sort of problem. On the other hand, they also suspected the father of intellectual retardation. Parents are accused precisely of being unable to look after children and take care of them.

As we can see, the main reason for withdrawal is a personal judgment. There is no objective evidence of harm done to the child. Here we must also add the fact that the children of immigrants are taken away more frequently. Perhaps this is because the immigrants themselves do not realize how careful they should be. Most immigrants, especially from Southern and Eastern Europe, are used to the fact that children are brought up by themselves, not by state institutions. The Norwegian mentality thus turns out to be foreign to them.

International scandals are not something that stays away from Barnevernet. The attempted child abduction led to diplomatic tensions with the Czech Republic and Poland. As Whewell reports, "One case involving a Czech family in Norway has led to a major diplomatic row between Norway and the Czech Republic. Czech President Milos Zeman accused Norwegian social workers of acting like Nazis" (Whewell par. 25). Usually, in such situations, immigrant families flee Norway before their children are forcibly taken away. But so far, Norway has not shown that it is heeding diplomatic pressure from other countries, including the Strasbourg Court.

The sad thing about this system is that the parents are guilty until proven guilty. They may be charged by any citizen of Norway; information may be brought to Norwegian social services for subjective reasons. But no one investigates the whistleblowers, nor the social workers themselves. Thus, Barnevernet exists as a state within a state, and we can safely say that it does not adhere to its main function - to keep

and protect children!

1.3 Children's removal from their families- psychological and legal dimensions

Summary:

Here we will discuss the psychological trauma caused to children by their

permanent separation from their families. We will also discuss the problem of the attitude

of the legislation to such removals. Every effort should be made to preserve a family

unless there is definite evidence of a crime being committed.

Speaking of children, we must mention that they get psychological trauma from

this separation. Even if it is temporary, even for a few days, they panic and think that

separation from their loved ones is imminent. Here we will refer to an article by

psychologist Shanta Trivedi that deals with this very aspect.

Trivedi begins his article with the thesis that "children also suffer complex and

long-lasting harms when they are removed from their parents and placed into foster care.

Yet, in most states, courts consider only whether a child is at risk of harm if she remains

in her parents' care" (Trivedi 526). Unfortunately, the court often feels that it possesses

the exclusive right to decide on behalf of the child. But does the court know what this

child wants, what he/she needs, and is he/she really being abused?

Whether or not there are grounds for taking a child away, the trauma of separation

remains (except, perhaps, in extreme cases of physical abuse). As Trivedi notes, "Due to their psychological attachments, children may long to return to their biological families after being placed with a foster family, even when their biological families previously mistreated them" (Trivedi 528). This is easily explained by the theory of attachment - a child is raised by certain people from a young age and, therefore, feels attached to them. It does not matter if they are parents or close relatives - unconsciously, this child stays with them for a very long time. That is why a separation should take place gradually, with the child's well-being in mind. A child should be able to see his/her family every day unless the parent(s) in question has committed a serious crime. But in the cases we discussed above, no such crime was committed.

Instead, we see the opposite process - a child is taken away without any prior indication, without anyone being warned. The difference between such removal and kidnapping is very small: "A child may be roused from their sleep, taken from their bed in the middle of the night, put into a car with strangers, and dropped into a holding center overnight until their removal is approved by a court and a foster care placement is identified" (Trivedi 531).

The authorities can justify themselves in the following way: if the parents find out that there is an investigation against them, they can easily go into hiding with their children. But how easy is it for a family to run away from the police just like that without leaving a trace? It is much more possible for an aggressive parent to run away alone, without their children. Moreover, in many cases of domestic violence, the mother manages to escape somewhere with her children. Why, then, should a child be taken away in the middle of the night? It is an operation that puts children in shock. From then on, they will have mental trauma, and no amount of compensation will clear it up.

As already mentioned, these investigations are carried out by social workers, not the police (unless there is evidence of a crime). The situation in America is no different from Norway in this regard: "There is a dire risk that caseworkers' subjective views of 'good parenting'... will determine whether or not a child is removed" (Trivedi 535). In a word, a social worker decides to take a child away at night because they believe there is a serious risk to the child's life. But if this decision is not justified, what happens? Who is responsible?

Nonetheless, all this does not end with adoption but rather begins with it. The most important thing for social workers is to take away a child without envisioning the life of that child later. There are reports that adoptive parents sometimes do not treat adopted children well. As Trivedi reports, "Despite the entire system being built on assumptions to the contrary, there is substantial evidence that children are more likely to be abused in foster care than in the general population" (Trivedi 542). And this is not an unjustified statement because it is supported by facts. So a myth needs to be debunked - adoptive parents do not always treat their children well.

Caring for children is expressed in a different way. Some children are abused, and others are simply neglected. Trivedi reports that "Foster parents may also neglect their foster children in less overt ways. In a survey of foster children, twenty-two percent reported that they were not getting enough food. Twenty-six percent revealed that they did not have appropriate seasonal clothing" (Trivedi 543). To all this, we can add the partial lack of control over adopted children, as a result of which they begin practices that are harmful and dangerous: "Foster children engage in sexual behavior at a younger age than their non-foster care counterparts. They are also more likely to engage in riskier sexual behavior such as unprotected sex. As a result, teenage pregnancy is higher in the foster care population" (Trivedi 548).

There is a logical explanation for this - very often, children in foster care spend their first months or years in less favorable conditions. With them, there is more stress, more conflicts. Different people take care of them, which makes it difficult for children to become permanently attached.

On the other hand, sometimes adoptive parents take excellent care of their children. Adoptive parents are often people who long to have children. That is why they also show serious concerns that even surpass normal concerns. We should not think that all adopted children show a tendency toward risky practices (alcohol, drugs, early sexual activity). But, as Trivedi reports, with them that risk is slightly greater. As we explained, this is due to the fact that they cannot form a lasting bond with a parent early in life and their first months are a period of great stress.

Trivedi criticized the federal authorities' apparent preference for taking children and giving them up for adoption. This principle, he argues, is wrong, but it is clearly visible in legislation and judicial practice. As Trivedi notes, "The federal government displayed a preference for adoption and therefore designed a system which favors removals, as children must first be taken from their biological families in order for them to be adopted later" (Trivedi 559). This is the basis of federal law as well as most state laws.

However, some states still try to track these children after they are taken from their biological parents. Trivedi writes that "Some states, like Maryland, require or allow a hearing after the child is placed in shelter care to determine whether it is contrary to the welfare of the child to return home" (Trivedi 561). This is the right policy in this case because sometimes a child's life away from his/her biological family can be even more difficult than before. We can only imagine the situation with the five "removed" children in Norway and how they would live far from each other. A child's life does not end when it is removed from social services. What follows is not paradise. The child will still experience problems and will have to deal with his/her traumas. And it is not always the best option to convince him/her that his/her parents are "bad" and incapable of looking after the child.

Here Trivedi addresses the legal aspect of the child removal problem. Yes, some states require consideration of the potential harm of removing children and separating them from their biological families. But despite this, it does not oblige judges to address this problem: "Even if lawyers make these arguments, judges are not required to take the information into account... No statutory guidance exists for weighing this evidence against any perceived risk of harm in keeping the child at home" (Trivedi 562). That is, three things must be present here: (1) legislation at the federal and state levels to allow consideration of potential harms from the removal of children, (2) an obligation for judges to consider those potential harms, and (3) legislation that clearly defines what happens if the harm of removal outweighs the benefits.

Another fact we should point out here is that a possible reunification of a given family is based on the interests of both the parents and the children: "While the right to family integrity was initially framed as belonging to the parents, Supreme Court jurisprudence suggests this right belongs to children, too." Referring to a specific court case from 1982, Trivedi notes that "In Santosky v. Kramer, the earliest expansion of the right to family integrity, the Court noted that, until a finding of unfitness, parents and children share an interest in preventing termination of their relationship" (Trivedi 563). From here, it logically follows that the need to separate the child from his/her parents must be proven; and in many cases, this does not happen. At the constitutional level, there is also such a requirement – "The Constitution arguably requires consideration of the harm of removal as a part of such balancing, because there is a fundamental liberty interest in the family unit and the bonds within it" (Trivedi 565).

As we can see, there is still much to be desired from legislation on both a federal and state basis. Consideration should be given to making judges legally compelled to consider the potential harm of family separation, and social workers being held accountable for their misjudgments. We cannot leave a fateful decision in the hands of an ordinary person who has some experience and education but may yield to his subjective feelings and judgment.

Here Trivedi relies on the case titled In re Rihana J.H., 147 A.D.3d 945. Because of an alleged injury inflicted on her brother Kaden, Rihana J.H. is separated from her mother. It is the assessment of social services that she may also be subject to abuse. The court is considering whether Rihanna should remain separated from her mother and brother. As Trivedi points out, "Ultimately, the court found that it did not need to resolve the issue of how Kaden's injury occurred to determine whether Rihana could reunite with her mother." For the court, these are two separate issues; therefore, "The court analyzed this case under Nicholson and noted that it must balance any risk of harm if Rihana was returned to her mother against the emotional and mental harm of her continued removal" (Trivedi 570).

Obviously, this case does not mean that children of a given family can be easily abused and the court leaves them to their parents. The question is, rather, where is the line between state and federal authorities and the family? What are the prerogatives of the authorities, and how far can they push the family? When can they restrict parental rights? In short, which of the two conceptions is closer to the best interests of the child - that of preserving the family or that of children belonging to the federal/state authorities?

For some time now, a movement to preserve the family has been gaining ground in this country. It strongly opposes the principle that a child should be quickly taken away from a parent. In an article from 1993, Marc Mannes reviews the development of this social movement. According to him, there is no precise and clear definition of what exactly is "movement for family preservation." Different views and ideas are combined in this movement. As Mannes notes, "Some academics and professionals choose to see the concept limited to short term intensive service programs that strive to prevent the out-of-home placement of children, while others adopt a more expansive family support orientation" (Mannes 5).

It is undeniable that this movement emerged as a resistance to the current "child protection" system. This system, as mentioned, is based on the principle that the authorities decide what is best for the child. Children are not seen as part of a family but as units that belong solely to society, i.e., they are "government-owned." As Mannes explains, "The Family Preservation Movement emerged in response to one particular structural strain on the social welfare delivery system- the failure to address the needs of vulnerable families and the resulting emphasis on out-of-home placements in foster care" (Mannes 8). This resistance is due to the fact that there are cases of abuse by federal and state agencies. As we have already seen, they do not always consider the interests of the child and sometimes solve a case according to their personal biases.

The main principle of this social movement is contained in the following words: "Every child should grow up in a permanent family... The best way to accomplish permanency is by working with all family members in order to preserve families and prevent the placement of children outside the home." This does not mean that parents have absolute rights over their children: "Family preservation accepts the fact there will be instances where substitute care is needed, but this option should only be exercised after all other viable alternatives have been exhausted" (Mannes 11).

Hence, it is important to work with parents and children to prevent family breakdown. This includes support for parents and children in crisis (for example, financial problems lead to stress and, accordingly, mental or physical abuse); observing how a family functions; financial and educational support for children. Undoubtedly, divorces are among the most significant difficulties in preserving a family, and the efforts of social workers should be aimed at preventing them.

It is also true that domestic violence also depends on the character of the specific perpetrator. There are people who are just aggressive, and nothing can stop that. That is why a family cannot be preserved at any cost. The point is, if there are such acts of violence, to react very quickly and the child stays together with his/her other parent, as well as brothers and sisters. It is not logical at all when there is an aggressive father, the mother to be separated from her child. What is her fault for this? Why should the child be subjected to a double trauma - first, physical abuse, and then mental trauma?

Every day we are told statistics about domestic crimes - and especially about murders in the family. *The purpose of this daily repetition of the same fact is to convince us that children are the property of the state.* In this way, the quick and sudden removal of children from both parents is justified. However, no one asks the question of why these children are taken away and sent to strangers instead of being placed in the care of their mother, uncle, aunt, grandmother or grandfather? Why should the children's relatives also suffer and not even have the opportunity to meet the child?

Here we must point to one more fact, which is hard to accept but true. Not everyone is suited to be a parent. There are parents who abuse alcohol, drugs, etc. There are also aggressive parents. There are parents who know little about raising children. This can hardly be changed. But if the emphasis is on establishing a system that works with such parents, the cases of domestic violence will decrease.

Additionally, we should not underestimate the role of globalization and consumerism, which dominate our society. Parents are busy, they do not have time for their children. They often ignore them in order to earn money and pursue a career. This is the disease of our time - we rush to accumulate material goods. Thus, the relationship with one's own children is lost, and that is where the problems begin. Children begin to go their own way, not trusting their parents. Then the breakup of the family is close, even if it is not officialized.

In relation to all this, legislators at the federal level passed three crucial bills: (1) the Family Preservation Act of 1990, (2) the Children and Family Services Act of 1990, (3) S.3174 (related to the Social Security Act). These legislative acts offer important insights on issues such as: "preplacement prevention, family preservation, reunification, and aftercare; established a new uncapped entitlement effort to offer intensive family-based crisis intervention programs for children at imminent risk of placement" (Mannes 18). Additionally, they launch a program to support and strengthen families in order to prevent them from falling apart. These bills have had some impact on keeping families together, but more efforts are needed today. Particularly this is true because there are forces eager to focus on the removal of children from their families. We need to oppose this tendency and be ready to stipulate the right of children to remain in their families as long as possible.

1.4 Conclusion

Today, as a result of the extreme measures taken by social services in America and elsewhere, the movement to preserve the family is becoming more extreme in turn. Thanks to social media, we can follow various legal cases and the fight of entire families with the authorities. Very often, representatives of this movement emphasize that children are almost always taken by force and without good reason. The truth is actually that we have a clash of the two conceptions mentioned earlier. There are parents that really abuse their children, or show neglect; but these parents cannot understand their mistake. On the contrary, there are social workers believing that parents cannot have any rights over their children. In this confrontation, it is necessary to find a compromise option: one that limits the rights of the parents only in the case of crimes committed by them, and at the same time, that really takes into account the interests and needs of the child. In any case, it is very rare for both parents to abuse or neglect their children. But even then, the children must be placed in the care of close relatives.

Who do children really belong to? Here we can already answer precisely and clearly: children are individuals that do not belong to anyone, but the task of raising them is very serious, and it should not be delegated to state institutions. The biological family is the right environment for children. The relationship with the mother begins after conception, and this should not be forgotten. In most cases, there is no reason for children to be separated from their mother either.

The concept of children "belonging" to the government dates back to Plato. His mistake is that he sees in all citizens only tools for the realization of some abstract idea. For him, this is the welfare of the state. But the idea of breaking up the family and raising children by a special group of women is harmful. They go against human nature.

In Norway we see the extremes that follow from this conception. Children are taken without reason in the middle of the night; they are separated from their parents for life, thus condemned to mental traumas to carry with them always.

Our conclusion is that our social services need to be reformed so that they look after the family rather than their own interest. We are U.S. citizens with all the rights that come with it. In the absence of an established crime, a child cannot be taken away - let alone because of "poverty" or because of "parental incapability." Therefore, a return to the basic constituent of society - the family - and full support for it is necessary.

But the problem of how far the government can interfere in family affairs remains. Now we are going to discuss another problem that is no less important.

Chapter II: Sex education

Having considered a very exciting and controversial issue - do children belong to their parents or to the state - it is now time to move on to another problem. Education is an essential part of our life and we cannot imagine a child without education. Every child is endowed with the right to education, because in this way, the child can develop knowledge and skills and realize themselves in life. There is no dispute about that. Regarding the content of the curricula, there are also not many disputes - natural sciences, humanities, and art are a must. But there are two controversial areas that still provoke heated debates - religion and sex/sexuality education.

Here we will focus on the question of what sexuality education is and what it should look like. First, we will introduce the reader to what this education is, and then we will identify two opposite approaches - the comprehensive approach and the abstinence approach. We will compare them and show which of these approaches is more suitable for our children.

2.1 What is sex education?

Summary:

Here we will introduce the problem of sex education in general- what is its history in the United States, why we need it at all, and in what form it exists today.

Human sexuality seems like a self-evident concept. We have no particular questions about it because we think we know everything. But that is not really the case. Sexuality is a very important part of our nature - something that is claimed by religious people and atheists alike. That is why we should not ignore it. In fact, sexuality is deeply connected to love and human relationships. The very existence of two sexes is related to sexuality. For atheists, it is the result of evolution; for religious people, it is the result of Our Creator's decision to give man (Adam) a companion and partner. In any case, one fact is certain: a man and a woman cannot do without each other.

Why do we even need to talk about sex education? Is this education and what exactly does it focus on?

The need for sex education is related to talking about sex and human sexuality. The fact is that with the advent of Christianity, the topic of sexuality was seriously ignored. There are both theological and cultural arguments for this. It was simply the spirit of the age - in the Middle Ages it was much more important to develop as a person, spiritually, than to concentrate on one's sexuality. Also, Christianity perceives sexuality in the context of sinfulness. Before Original Sin, sexuality did not exist, at least not in the current sense of the word. There were two sexes, but they were in a different type of relationship with each other. This is explained in a document published by the Sacred congregation for Catholic education: "Since men and women in their time have been inclined to reduce sexuality to genital experience alone, there have been reactions tending to devalue sex, as though by its nature men and women were defiled by it" (Congregation sect. 28). Christianity is opposed to the pagan attitude that perceives human nature as controlled by passions, with no need to control it. The concept of the family of

Christianity is based on monogamy, which was de facto denied, for example, in Ancient Greece. This is also why human sexuality is ignored.

Undoubtedly, with the dominance of the worldview of materialism, with the emergence of evolutionary theory and psychoanalysis, the West began to pay more attention to sexuality. This is a kind of compensation where scientists literally fixate on this topic. One of the first scientists to do this was the Austrian psychologist and psychiatrist Sigmund Freud. He placed sexuality at the heart of his psychoanalysis, according to which all our mental problems stem from the repression of sexual desire. But Freud understood the latter as a wild instinct that should not be controlled and should simply be allowed to run rampant.

Gradually, interest in sexuality increased and all kinds of materials were now freely published. The sexual revolution that began in the 1960s completed this process. We can safely say that this is the complete antithesis of the Christian worldview and the Christian approach to human sexuality.

Sexuality education today is seen as focusing entirely on the physiological aspects of this human phenomenon. Instead, it should be considered more broadly, as explained in the document "Educational Guidance in Human Love. Outlines for Sex Education" (1983): "Sexuality characterizes man and woman not only on the physical level, but also on the psychological and spiritual... Such diversity, linked to the complementarity of the two sexes, allows thorough response to the design of God" (Congregation sect. 5).

In speaking of these rapid changes, it is well to turn to a brief summary of the history of sex education in America. It will help us understand where we are now and what exactly has changed in the definition of this type of education. For this purpose, we will refer to an article by Valerie Huber and Michael Firmin (2014).

As early as the second half of the 19th century, the idea of sexual education existed, and it aimed to make young people know more about marriage and prepare them for it. At the end of the 19th century, the notion of gender equality appeared, which partly affected intimate relations between men and women. More interesting is the emergence of the Hygienic Movement, which sought to clarify the causes of various diseases and how to protect the citizens from them. In general, sexuality is associated with either marriage or STDs. We call this era progressive.

As noted by Huber and Firmin, "During the progressive era, the public discussion of sex always stressed sexual abstinence until marriage. Sex generally was seen as a function primarily for procreation, particularly among eugenists." However, in the 1920s Margaret Sanger pointed to pleasure as a function of sex (Huber and Firmin 28). Between these two points of view, however, stand two important events: the training of American soldiers during World War I and the Chicago Experiment.

As the researchers note, during The First World War, American soldiers were educated about sexually transmitted diseases (STD). They were warned not to enter any casual relationship since this could lead to difficulties on the battlefield. The infected ones were isolated or even jailed, and the ones without STD were praised and got rewards. Huber and Firmin report that "The War Department (1918) sought to continue the progress made with servicemen by giving them a book upon leaving the military. It encouraged returning soldiers to instruct their younger brothers on the dangers of venereal disease" (Huber and Firmin 30). Here we also see clearly what the attitude toward sex education was during this period: it had to prevent the dissemination of STDs. As we can see, this is a very important problem, which is still part of educational programs in schools today.

Speaking of Freud, we should mention that his ideas gained popularity in the United States as well. Shortly before the beginning of the First World War, Freud was already a famous and popular scientist. Fewer and fewer scientists and intellectuals laughed at his ideas (about the power of the sexual instinct, neurosis as caused by lack of sexual activity, the Oedipus complex, etc.). So, in Chicago, where the famous Chicago School was established (with a considerable influence in the field of psychology and pedagogy), an attempt was made to give three lectures on sexuality. Lectures had to be presented to local students. Nevertheless, the attempt failed due to massive protests. It was thought that such lectures would strengthen immorality (Huber and Firmin 32).

We do not know precisely what would have happened if these lectures had actually been given in 1913. Their content would hardly have been very immoral. But it is a fact that society at that moment was not prepared for this topic. As we have already noted, sexuality was ignored for a long time precisely because it was viewed purely physiologically.

The First World War fundamentally changed our world, our worldview. The belief in rationality that preceded this war completely collapsed. People started paying more attention to their emotions, passions. They began to seek more pleasure; the secular beginning dominated, the religious principle was gradually (though not completely) marginalized. Women and men were no longer separated in school; meetings between unmarried couples became more frequent; more romance fiction books were also appearing. A new morality appeared, about which the authors write the following: "The new morality of the 1920s provided a window into the changing values among a significant number of young people. Sex and the liberal consumption of other vices were becoming increasingly commonplace" (Huber and Firmin 34).

Obviously, this morality was still very far from the "sexual revolution." In the 1920s and 1930s, there were many social and moral norms that are rarely enforced today. It was very rare to see pictures of naked men or women; erotic ads did not exist at all; there was strict control over the content of movies and theater plays. Certain books were prohibited for students and the latter did not have access to them.

That is when a "scientist," Alfred Kinsey, in the 1940s and 1950s published books discussing various issues of sexuality. As Huber and Firmin report, he even recorded couples having sex. His books were banned by many communities. Meanwhile, he was the first to claim that 10% of the population is homosexual (Huber and Firmin 34). These shocking publications began to gain popularity after World War II. This "scientist" remains a pioneer in his field, with his work foreshadowing what would happen some 30 years later.

World War II also changed many things for us. In a world of ruin, man searches for his new values. People decided they needed to stick more to material goods. The age of consumerism came upon us. Scientism (as a worldview based entirely on science) was beginning to dominate our society. Ethical hedonism was coming slowly but surely.

Sexual education in the 1950s was transformed to include issues related to marriage and cohabitation. It was still centered on the family, but it now included new themes that were becoming fashionable because of feminism. This huge change occurred in the 1960s, when the hippie movement appeared, and the counterculture took the hearts

of many people. The hippie movement was a reaction to the Vietnam War. It was a

branch of socialism, which, however, does not aim at class struggle or social revolution.

Hippies emphasized living together in one large community and the idea that pleasure is

an integral part of our lives.

Greater was the influence of the birth control pill, which was officially legalized

in America in 1960. It allowed the indulgence of pleasure without thinking about the

future. Young people were not worried about unwanted pregnancy. An additional factor

in the intensification of the sexual revolution was the legalization of abortion (Huber and

Firmin 38). All this resulted in the introduction of new ideas and principles in sex

education.

Sex education became more comprehensive but was also opposed by different

groups. All the while this "revolution" was going on, groups of defenders of traditional

values protested. They believed that exposing children and young people to pornography

is dangerous and harmful to both the individual and society. All this will lead to the

disintegration of the family, they thought. At that point, conservatives were against sex

education altogether.

After all, conservatives realized that it is impossible to fight the agenda behind

sex education. So they set out to transform it. As noted by Huber and Firmin, in the early

1980s no one was against sex education; but conservatives wanted this education to

include only the prevention of STDs and unwanted pregnancy. At that time, the approach

that today we call abstinence education was developed. Government institutions started allocating money for training in this approach, with government funding halted recently by Barack Obama.

During that time, for about 30 years, two parallel systems of sex education have existed in America: comprehensive education and abstinence education. The first is based on the assumption that children and young people need to know all the details about sexuality. This approach emphasizes physiology.

The other approach emphasizes the need to prevent venereal diseases and unwanted pregnancies. Neither approach gains precedence through legislation at the federal level. Individual school districts can define the content of sexuality education in school.

These two approaches are quite different from each other because of their different aims (although some of the content of this education is identical in both approaches). Valerie Huber and Michael Firmin point out that "Sex education advocates of the 1960s called for 'safe sex' or so-called comprehensive sex education, which permitted a continuation of sexual freedom, as long as contraception was used" (Huber and Firmin 40). This approach is so radical that it causes outrage among parents, teachers, and various organizations. It is supported by various NGOs, which these authors mention: "Advocacy groups such as SIECUS, Advocates for Youth, and Planned Parenthood receive significant funding from influential foundations, as well as from the federal government" (Huber and Firmin 43).

Today's situation is this: we have two approaches, but they are unequal in terms of budget and media coverage. Undoubtedly, comprehensive education enjoys a considerable advantage because it is promoted by "scientists," politicians, NGOs, media, and even Hollywood. Therefore, we will try to make a comparison of these two approaches.

However, before proceeding further, we will refer to the official WHO definition of sexuality education. In the document titled "Standards for Sexuality Education in Europe," formulated by WHO-Europe, we find the following definition: "Sexuality education means learning about the cognitive, emotional, social, interactive and physical aspects of sexuality" (WHO 20). The problem, however, is that behind this definition there is a hidden agenda, or an attempt to propagate a certain worldview. And all this is hidden under the name of "education." Let's take a closer look at what it is all about.

2.2 The comprehensive approach

Summary:

Here we show the basic principles of this approach. We refer to publications from the WHO, European parliament, Advocates for Youth, and other sources. The problem with this approach is that it involves covert LGBT propaganda. Also, it *encourages* students instead of warning them about possible threats of sexual activity.

The first approach to which we will turn now is the comprehensive approach. It is called so because it emphasizes the physiological features of human sexuality. In fact, it should be called *encouraging approach* because it does nothing but encourage young people to have sex. Of course, this is just a quibble over words, but the reader should keep in mind that certain approaches do not live up to their name. In this case it is exactly so - the name of this approach is neutral, but the content of this type of education is not neutral at all.

The comprehensive approach is based on the principle that children should know as much about sexuality as their age allows. The more they know, the more they will be able to protect themselves from venereal diseases and unwanted pregnancy.

Here we will refer to several publications that will clarify the essence of the comprehensive approach. The first of them is published by the organization Advocates for Youth. Their name also sounds innocent, but in fact they defend the "right" of young people to know everything possible about sex, in great detail. In one of their pamphlets on the facts and myths of comprehensive education, they define several important points that will allow us to better understand the essence of this approach.

These "Advocates" argue that the comprehensive approach is based on certain values and is not aimed purely at a single physiological activity. According to the Advocates, "Quality comprehensive sexuality education supports a rights-based approach in which values such as respect, acceptance, tolerance, equality, empathy, and reciprocity are inextricably linked to universally agreed human rights" (Advocates 1). In short, all these values are part of the approach in question. At first glance, everything seems quite normal, but let's go further and see the particular form of these values.

According to the Advocates, this approach offers sex education to different ages according to their needs and abilities. This education should start from kindergarten because young children also need information on specific topics from the intimate sphere: "In kindergarten through second grade, students learn about family structure, the proper names for body parts and what to do if someone touches them inappropriately"

(Advocates 2). Then, from three through eighth grade, pupils learn gradually about puberty, HIV, relationships, etc. As the Advocates claim, emphasis is put on abstinence. Then, high-school students "are provided more complete information about sexually transmitted infections and pregnancy, abstinence, and contraception and condoms. Students learn about relationships, develop healthy communication and responsible decision-making skills" (Advocates 2).

It is somewhat debatable to what extent there is an emphasis on abstinence here. Do 5th graders need to learn about AIDS at all? Aren't they still too young for information like that? It is assumed that at this age, they do not have sexual contacts. The risk of contracting HIV is very low. Shouldn't venereal diseases be discussed later? Of course, the idea of learning about puberty during these years is excellent because it prepares students well. And yet, it is important what exactly is taught about puberty - it is one thing to talk about how a child becomes an adult by going through this period; it is quite another to emphasize human physiology and the possibility of having sex at that age.

Contrary to the words that this education focuses on abstinence, a little further we read that abstinence education is harmful. As we read, "Abstinence-only programs marginalize young people who are already engaged in sexual relationships...These programs normalize stereotypes and promote images that are discriminatory because they are based on heteronormativity" (Advocates 2).

The problem for defenders of this approach is not the principle of celibacy until marriage. Their problem, as we see here, is "heteronormativity." What does this term mean?

"Heteronormativity" is a term coined by advocates of LGBT practices. According to them, we live in a world where it is considered acceptable for a man to marry a woman, not a man for a man or a woman for a woman. However, these LGBT promoters think that this is just a result of convention and not the natural course of things. In short, people once made up their minds that only relationships between men and women are considered normal, without having any basis for it.

So what does this concept have to do with comprehensive education? This approach necessarily includes information about homosexuality and LGBT people in general. This information is based on the principle of tolerance and empathy. In short, children are taught that it is natural to be LGBT and that anyone who does not like LGBT people is "immoral" and "intolerant."

And this is precisely the severe problem with this type of education - children are taught that there are "different people," that there are "different sexual orientations," and that they should be tolerant of LGBT people. And this is something that cannot be missed by the Advocates- as if sexual orientation is the most important thing for a child to learn!

Another topic on which Advocates are particularly emotional is the issue of contraception. According to them, sex education should teach young people to use contraception. They write that "Comprehensive sexuality education affirms the right of couples and individuals to voluntarily decide the size and spacing of their families. In developing countries, more than 215 million women are not using modern contraception" (Advocates 3). But it is one thing to learn and quite another to encourage and promote. In this case, we are talking about encouraging promiscuity among young people, this being combined with contraception. Once again, we see how an otherwise noble idea degenerates because of the already formed agenda behind modern comprehensive education.

In another document developed by the European Parliament, more important points are formulated that represent the essence of comprehensive education. In the publication titled "Comprehensive Sexuality Education: Why is it Important?" (2022), a number of reasons are given for choosing this approach.

As stated in that document, E.U. countries have different approaches to sexuality education. In some countries, it is mandatory by law, and in others, it is optional. In some countries, it necessarily includes LGBT themes, while in others, it does not. In the document, we read the following: "Considerable variation in the content, delivery and objectives of sexuality education still exists. Administrative decentralization plays an important role in financing and decision-making" (EP 37). Sex education in Western Europe is different from post-communist countries, where it is highly restricted and usually taught in biology classes.

Here is an example of this difference between Western and Eastern Europe. In the West, it is mandatory to talk about the relations between sexes, gender roles, gender perspectives. In short, it enters the field of sociology and cultural studies. In post-communist countries, this is not the case at all, and sex education is reduced to some basic facts about venereal diseases, human anatomy, and contraception. According to the authors of this document, "Sexuality education and gender equality are closely interwoven. Gender equality is both part of the content of sexuality education, as well as one of its key outcomes" (EP 40). We already see an ideological principle clearly expressed here: we must talk about the relations between sexes in the context of their equality. It must be emphasized that there are many stereotypes about women. And that is a fact: but is there some ulterior motive here?

Perhaps there is something not overtly said in such a formulation. From the notion of "stereotypes" we can easily arrive at the view that "gender does not exist" and it is only a "social construction." At school, it is mandatory to learn that the sexes are equal - at least, it is so in America and Europe. Why should we emphasize a truth that is not only written in the constitutions of many countries but also works in practice? There is clearly something else behind it. Where in the Western world is there gender discrimination both in law and in practice? We can guess it is not about gender equality. The real reason is that children need to learn "there are many genders" and that gender is something "fluid," not fixed.

However, the authors of this document are dissatisfied with the state of LGBT propaganda in the European Union. As they note, "Only a few EU Member States focus on topics related to gender in their sexuality education programs... For example, in Ireland, it was not compulsory for education curricula to include content on sexual orientation and gender identity" (EP 41). Here they state quite frankly what they want: that children in the E.U. learn more about "gender identity" so that they accept "gender re-assignment" and "non-binary people" as normal. And all this must happen in school!

As reported by the authors of this paper, only France, the Netherlands, and Sweden mandated the topic of LGBT to be included in the curricula (EP 58). And yet, the subject is not touched upon enough, as the authors complain. For example, in Sweden "LGBTI+ content is visible in all sexuality education chapters of biology textbooks, but sexual orientation is often constructed as fixed and stereotypical gender binaries are reinforced via heteronormative assumptions" (EP 59). This sounds strange because Sweden is one of the pioneers in promoting LGBT ideology. As we will see a little later, an experiment is being done in Swedish kindergartens - children are not separated by gender and play with the toys of the other gender. So this criticism does not seem legit. And why do we need to cover topics like sexual orientation in sex education classes at all?

The authors also complain that in Eastern Europe, more emphasis is placed on the biological and physiological dimensions of sexuality. For example, young people in Slovakia "ascribe greater importance to the physiological, psychological and relationship aspects of sexuality than to its social and cultural dimensions... Sexuality education in Slovak schools consists predominantly of biological and medical information" (EP 54). We can object thus: if the young people want such an education, why shouldn't they get it? Maybe they just do not want to talk about the "cultural dimensions of sexuality," i.e., "gender identity"?

The criticism of the current situation in Eastern Europe goes on with reference to conservative movements that specifically oppose the LGBT agenda in school: "There is strong opposition to sexuality education... This opposition strongly rejects sexual and gender diversity, both core components of comprehensive sexuality education, and emphasizes 'heteronormative' family values and 'restoring the Natural Order' (EP 68). Examples of this are the movements in Poland, Hungary, and Romania.

From all this, we are left with the impression that *sex education today does not deal with significant issues. It is simply a means of spreading the LGBT ideology* among young people, and besides, it is mandatory! How else can we explain all these criticisms?

As we can see, even in Eastern Europe, there is sex education, and young people there think that it satisfies their educational needs. Why should it be expanded further and controversial issues like "gender identity" be added? And when advocates of comprehensive education say that even Sigmund Freud wanted mandatory sex education among young people, why is it not mentioned that Freud would never have endorsed such a concept as "gender identity"?

Now it is time to turn to another interesting document. It was published by the WHO- Europe. It is called "Standards for Sexuality Education in Europe" (2010). In this document, we see various instructions to teachers, educators, NGOs regarding sex education classes in school and even kindergarten. Some of the notes we find here are outrageous.

The approach of the authors of these Standards is controversial. According to them, this education should start with the birth of every child! As they claim, "From birth, babies learn the value and pleasure of bodily contact, warmth and intimacy. Soon after that, they learn what is 'clean' and what is 'dirty.' Later, they learn the difference between male and female, and between intimates and strangers." The authors add that "from birth, parents in particular send messages to their children that relate to the human body and intimacy. In other words, they are engaging in sexuality education" (WHO 13).

The last sentence contains some truth; yes, parents can really talk to their children about the human body, about why there are women and men in this world. But this is a decision of the parents themselves, not of any non-governmental organization! If parents want, they will talk to their child about these things in the child's early years. Nonetheless, that is still up to them. This fact was ignored by the WHO team! According to them, parents are simply deprived of the right to talk with their children about sexuality.

Quite logically, the authors continue with the conception of comprehensive education. Their definition of this type of education is as follows: "Comprehensive sexuality education seeks to equip young people with the knowledge, skills, attitudes and values they need to determine and enjoy their sexuality - physically and emotionally, individually and in relationships." As we can see, the purpose of this education is to create a positive (i.e., encouraging) attitude about sex. That is why they add the following: "Young people need to be given the opportunity to acquire essential life skills and develop positive attitudes and values" (WHO 20).

It is not very clear exactly what skills are needed in this field. Maybe it is about handing out condoms to young people, or maybe some more specific advice? Certainly not a good thing, considering other interesting comments made in this post.

Now we come to the most controversial moment. This is a very interesting table of skills and knowledge that children should have at a given age. Shortly before that, the authors from the WHO substantiated their thesis that children should be "sexually educated" from an early age. According to them, young children simply need this: "Children have sexual feelings even in early infancy. Between the second and third year of their lives, they discover the physical differences between men and women." And now comes the most interesting part: "During this time children start to discover their own bodies (early childhood masturbation, self-stimulation) and they may also try to examine the bodies of their friends (playing doctor)" (WHO 23).

There is hardly any point in commenting on the last quote. This is not only enormous stupidity but also terrible cynicism. What kind of "masturbation" can we talk about here? And why should we address this phenomenon exactly? It seems that teachers should provide information specifically about masturbation. But these students are not 18-year-olds; these are six years old pupils just out of kindergarten!

Quite logically, in a table about the knowledge and skills of children, which it is DESIRABLE for them to have, it is written that children between 4-6 years should learn about "enjoyment and pleasure when touching one's own body; early childhood masturbation" (WHO 40).

It is not very clear what the defenders of comprehensive education will answer now. Is it normal to talk about such a topic with small children? The theory of this phenomenon in children dates back to Freud, but it has not been proven. Freud only said that young children have a "latent sexuality." This means that there are some signs that speak of sexuality in them, but that is about it. For example, finger-sucking is the typical gesture, according to Freud (although this is more related to breastfeeding, and accordingly, to the pleasure principle formulated by Freud).

Now we can already see what their aim is: to teach children from an early age that sex is normal and that they can practice it however and whenever they want. As they become teenagers, they will have no obstacles and will only want to practice what they have been "taught" to do. We will not even mention the possible consequences of all this if these children end up with a pedophile teacher, which sometimes happens. We do not want to think that the WHO wants to do something for the benefit of pedophiles, so we assume that their aim is something else. But whatever that aim is, it remains arrogant and cynical. Children are neither "sexual subjects" nor "sexual objects," and that it is! There is nothing more to add here.

But this is not the end of our analysis of comprehensive education. Here we will refer to another instance of the extremes to which the advocates of this education go. We are already receiving information about cases of schools that promote LGBT quite officially. There are classes there that talk about LGBT issues. But in Europe, things go to an absolute extreme. In Sweden, a peaceful northern country with a high standard of living, some kindergartens have introduced "gender-neutral education."

Here we turn to an article by Ellen Barry from 2018. She describes the behavior of teachers in a kindergarten that was conducting a "gender neutral" experiment. At the beginning of the experiment, the children played their gender roles according to the "stereotypes"- boys are violent and aggressive, girls are meek and cannot say "no." As Barry writes, "The boys were clamorous and physical. They shouted and hit. The girls held up their arms and whimpered to be picked up. The group of 1- and 2-year-olds had, in other words, split along traditional gender lines. And at this school, that is not O.K." (Barry par. 2).

The manager of the kindergarten decides to start an experiment - what will happen to the children if they are not addressed as a girl or a boy? What if they could choose their own toys without any prior division? Will the behavior of all the children change?

Currently, the conception of "gender self-determination" is being promoted throughout Sweden. According to this view, each child can define their gender, which sometimes may not match their biological sex. As this author writes, "It is normal, in

many Swedish preschools, for teachers to avoid referring to their students' gender —
instead of 'boys and girls,' they say 'friends,' or call children by name. Play is organized
to prevent children from sorting themselves by gender" (Barry par. 5). Even a "gender-
neutral pronoun" was introduced.

As might be expected, not scientists stand at the heart of this experiment, but
lobbyists. All this began with the activity of a journalist: "Sweden's experiment in
gender-neutral preschools began in 1996 in Trodje... The man who started it, Ingemar
Gens, was not an educator but a journalist who dabbled in anthropology and gender
theory" (Barry par. 11). In a word, a journalist who considers himself a scientist (without
grounds) decides to start an experiment, imposing on children a pattern that is contrary to
nature.

One teacher shared that she finds it difficult to follow the "new model," but she
manages it anyway. She thinks the model is effective, and indeed some girls are
becoming bolder and some boys are starting to play with 'toys for girls.' Here the author
gives an example of 3-year-old Otto: "Otto prefers to wear dresses because he likes the
way they fan out when he spins around... Up until now, no one in Otto's life... has told
him that boys don't wear dresses, said his mother, Lena Christiansson, 36, matter-of-
factly" (Barry par. 35).

Is there anything good about a 3-year-old boy being encouraged to wear dresses?
Yes, the correct word is "encouraged." This boy is just following his mother's lead and
dressing like her. That is where his passion for dresses comes from. There is probably an
absentee father in this family. In any case, someone should tell him that boys wear pants;
there is nothing scary in telling this fact.

Of course, just because Otto dresses like this does not mean he is going to change his gender. This may be a temporary fad that will fade after kindergarten. The problem is that *there is no neutrality* here. The child is simply encouraged and motivated to do this. Society encourages him, because this child is a great example of "Swedish tolerance." And Swedes need to feel "tolerant."

But within society itself, critical voices are also emerging. The author notes the following: "A columnist and mathematician named Tanja Bergkvist, one of the few figures who routinely attacks what she calls 'Sweden's gender madness,' says many Swedes are uncomfortable with the practice but are afraid to criticize it in public" (Barry par 26). And this is not very surprising - when an ideology dominates a society, it is very difficult to stand against it. This is especially true when it is imposed by the country's political and economic elite. In Sweden, the LGBT dogma cannot be questioned; everything LGBT advocates say should be taken as absolutely true. And so it turns out that if you are naming boys and girls the right, natural way, you are actually wrong!

The last example shows well what the real problem with comprehensive education is. It is all because of promoting LGBT propaganda among children. There is absolutely no need for children to know more about homosexuality, "gender identity," etc. They can discuss this with their parents. Then they can count on having different points of view. And when "sexual orientation" is discussed in school, homosexuality is always viewed in a positive way, as something good and even acceptable.

Another major weakness of this approach is encouraging young people to have sex. Sex is only talked about as a good thing, without its possible difficulties. Very often, teachers do not explain at all that teenagers are not ready for sex, both physically and mentally. What they do not explain is that people having sex should be responsible for the potential outcome of it, i.e., pregnancy. Undoubtedly, encouraging sexual activity among young people also increases the number of abortions. Abstaining from sex leads to the opposite - to a decrease in their number.

Our third objection to this approach is obvious. Sex education in our schools is often conducted by "external experts." These are people working for a given NGO. They create the content of this education and are engaged in teaching. In many cases, these are not even people with teaching experience! In our opinion, only teachers and especially biology specialists should deal with this. It is from this that the NGO educators in question talk more about "gender identity" than the most important issues related to sexuality. They simply lack knowledge of the physiological dimensions of sexuality!

And our last, fourth objection says this: parents should have a say! All children under the age of 16 should be closely supervised by their parents, and any sexual activity should be discouraged. *A teacher cannot tell a 13-year-old how to have safe sex.* It should be the exact opposite - to talk about the problems ensuing from sexual activity; that he/she should abstain until a certain age. Yes, some children at this age are already sexually active, but this is already a problem for their parents to solve. They should not be encouraged under any circumstances!

So, we came to the following concluding points: sex education should (1) focus on sexual abstinence, (2) leave the more serious topics to parents, (3) not be provided by "external experts," and (4) to also focus on love and family, because *human sexuality has its function, and that is precisely the creation of a family.* In this way, we can safely move on to consider the other approach – the approach of abstinence.

2.3 The abstinence approach

Summary:

Here we look at the basic principles of abstinence education. We will refer to the Catholic doctrine of sexuality education as part of the knowledge of the family. We will show why comprehensive education is not enough. We will offer a list of the main principles of abstinence education.

Many people mistakenly view sex education as only encouraging sexual activity. But there is actually another approach that needs to be known more about. This is the alternative approach, which is called abstinence education. At its core, there is the assumption that *children should learn about sex only in the context of the family*; and that means they have to be motivated to abstain from sex until they are ready to establish a family.

Here we will refer to two documents: the document published by the Sacred Congregation for Catholic Education titled "Educational Guidance in Human Love. Outlines for Sex Education," and an article by Alean Zeiler (2014) regarding abstinence education. From them, we will learn what are the basic principles of the so-called abstinence education.

In the first document, we see various views related to the education of children in general. Sexual education should be seen in its holistic aspect - it is part of the upbringing of children. We cannot raise our children without considering the most important human activities - family, love, friendship. It is clear that most advocates of comprehensive education do not much like the idea of the traditional family, or the family in general. It is also clear that they emphasize pleasures more than responsibility. But abstinence education focuses on the latter; that is why we can also call it *responsibility education.*

In this document from 1983, it is noted that at that time a number of Catholic organizations already "have begun to carry out a positive work of sex education; it is directed not only to help children and adolescents on the way to psychological and spiritual maturity, but also and above all to protect them from the dangers of ignorance and widespread degradation" (Congregation sect. 12). In short, sex education is necessary precisely to show the danger of debauchery and sexual activity that starts too early. Children need advice and support to cope with these dangers. They mistakenly think that sexual activity is pure pleasure.

The biggest mistake regarding sex is to perceive it as something in itself, without connection with love. The existence of two sexes, as stated in this document, is the work of God; God made us men and women for a purpose. This purpose is to be able to reproduce, to create a family, and also to complement each other. As it says further, "The human person, through his or her intimate nature, exists in relation to others, implying a reciprocity of love. The sexes are complementary: similar and dissimilar at the same time; not identical" (Congregation sect. 25). We must complement and help each other; in addition, we have different functions in creating the family - the woman becomes pregnant and gives birth, and then nurses her child, and the man participates in the conception, and then takes care of his pregnant wife and later of his young child. These roles and functions are not interchangeable.

The family should be the primary focus of sexuality education. Therefore, perhaps the most correct name for this subject would be Family education. Such a subject would give more information about life in general; children will know more about what the roles of the mother and father are, what their relationship is with the child, what is a family budget, how to maintain a lasting relationship in the family, why some parents are alone, why some children are abandoned, what is adoption, etc.

Of course, from a Catholic point of view, all this must be put into the context of Catholic doctrine: about our relationship with God, the meaning of our earthly existence, marriage as a sacrament, etc. In this regard, parents can also get involved: "The full realization of conjugal life and, in consequence, the sanctity and stability of the family, depend on the formation of conscience and on values assimilated during the whole formative cycle of the parents themselves" (Congregation sect. 52). This subject should be part of family education, i.e., this is where school and family meet.

At the end of the document, we also see a critique of sex education as it was in the 1980s. The purpose of this education must be completely different from what is presented today in school: "Sex education is not reducible to simple teaching material, nor to theoretical knowledge alone... but it has a specific objective in view: that affective maturation of the pupil, of self control, and of correct behavior in social relationships" (Congregation sect. 70). In short, it is education in good manners and morals.

Modern sex education is harmful to children for many reasons. Learning content must be carefully selected and filtered. There are things that are not allowed in school, no matter what the age of the students. As written in this document, "Some school text-books on sexuality, by reason of their naturalist character, are harmful to the child and the adolescent. Graphic and audio-visual materials are more harmful when they crudely

present sexual realities for which the pupil is not prepared" (Congregation sect. 76).

Today, we see precisely that in school: erotic pictures, models of genitalia, and even

"games" with condoms! This should not be allowed, at least for students under the age of

16. These materials can lead to a distorted view of sex and human relationships in

general. They turn a person into a sexual object rather than a person. Therefore, they

should also be avoided, and the information to be given verbally. And shocking images

(for example, a sexual act) should be absolutely prohibited in school.

This document provides only some directions for development in the field of

sexuality education. Now we will turn to an interesting article about abstinence

education. Alcan Zeiler points to early sexual activity as doing great harm to teenagers.

According to this author, we cannot convey information about sex to them in an entirely

positive way. Teenagers have a serious problem with unwanted pregnancy and venereal

diseases, but that is not all: "Even if sexually active teens escape acquiring STIs and

becoming pregnant, few remain emotionally unscathed. Overall, one in eight teens suffers

from depression, and suicide has risen to become the third leading cause of death for

adolescents" (Zeiler 373). This means that the mental traumas are by no means small.

Why isn't this talked about in school?

Unwanted pregnancy is something that cannot be avoided with contraception

alone. Whatever measures two young people take, they cannot be absolutely sure. Yes,

contraception gives a little more "safety," but young people tend to overestimate it. There

is only one way out of this situation: "Abstaining from all sexual activity is the only 100

percent safe and effective way to avoid teen pregnancies, STIs, and the emotional fallout of adolescent sexual activity." Then she adds that "Almost 40 years of emphasis on 'safer sex' with 'values-neutral sex education,' condoms and contraception has clearly failed our young people" (Zeiler 373). This is what we have called "encouraging education" - instead of warning young people, they are encouraged with no clear purpose.

Notwithstanding, in sex education classes, it is not taught that condoms are not absolutely safe and often not even effective. Therefore, such a subject is needed, which clearly states there are threats to young people if they are sexually active and do not have only one partner. We do not have to stand completely against condoms: "Abstinence education curricula, however, do not discourage the use of condoms; rather they note that chastity obviates the need for condoms. Abstinence education programs do not claim that condoms have no place in preventing STIs" (Zeiler 374). Having one permanent partner reduces the risk of sexually transmitted diseases as well as unwanted pregnancy; in case of pregnancy, the couple must decide to keep the child. This is exactly what young people need to understand - they have a huge responsibility, and sex is not just pure pleasure.

Another comment from this article that we need to address concerns the role of the sexually encouraging non-governmental organization called SIECUS. It is an organization that spreads material harmful to the mentality and morals of young people. As Zeiler reports, "the American College of Pediatricians recommends that parents be fully aware of the content of the curriculum to which their children are being exposed." The National Guidelines developed by SIECUS are the object of hot debates within our society: "According to these guidelines, children between the ages of 5 to 8 years should be taught not only the anatomically correct names of all body parts, but also the definitions of sexual intercourse, and masturbation" (Zeiler 374). This is the same idea that we noted earlier as being present in similar instructions from the WHO - that there is no problem with kindergarten children learning about masturbation.

The very name "abstinence education" is wrong because this approach to sex education includes much more than abstinence. As Zeiler notes, "Programs that teach sexual abstinence until marriage are about much more than simply delaying sexual activity. They assist adolescents in establishing positive character traits, formulating long-term goals, and developing emotionally healthy relationships" (Zeiler 375). Sex education should be part of a subject dedicated to the family. As the author adds, "These programs increase the likelihood of strong marriages and families—the single most essential resource for the strength and survival of our nation" (Zeiler 375).

In view of all these observations, we can make the following list of the most important principles of abstinence education:

1. Focus on the family - relations between parents, parents and children; knowledge of how to build a family.

2. Description of various problems related to sex- venereal diseases, unwanted pregnancy, mental trauma, sexual abuse.

3. Encouraging young people to seek a stable, lasting relationship with a permanent partner.

4. Avoiding topics and materials unsuitable for children under 16. Absolute prohibition of pornographic images.

5. Sex education starts at a minimum of 12 years. Before that, children may learn more about the family and partly about human anatomy (within science lessons).

6. Only the experts are teachers - mostly specialists in biology, medicine and psychology. "External experts" that specialize in "gender studies" are not to enter the classroom.

7. Full consent from the parents for their children's participation in these classes. Prior approval of course content. Parents possibly attending some classes, if they wish.

These are the principles that any sex education should adhere to. They are based on common sense, morality, the public interest and the interest of children. It is hard to repudiate any of these points.

With all this in mind, we should fight for federal funding allocated for activities defined by this approach. This funding still exists at the moment but it is too little compared to the funding of the alternative approach. But it is not all about funding. We are inundated daily with information about how "harmful" the abstinence approach is, which we call here the family or personal responsibility approach. It is very difficult to even come across scientific publications that look at this approach positively.

Undeniably, there is censorship on this issue. Major scientific journals and universities in the United States greenlight only the other approach. Accordingly, this is used by its defenders to justify its extensive funding and complete disregard for the family approach. And it turns out that ordinary people do not know much about this approach. They think it is either "harmful" or unrelated to sex education. And this is not the case at all!

Funding for the comprehensive approach comes mostly from foundations and NGOs. That should tell us something: someone is behind all of this. As already mentioned, *there is a hidden agenda behind sex education classes in school.* In these classes, they talk about LGBT people, about the fact that we should be tolerant of such people, and children are even encouraged to change their gender if they so desire. All this is not accidental, nor is it the result of anyone's benevolence and "good heart." These issues should be discussed at home. If the parents decide they want to, let them talk about LGBT people. This is not the job of schools, foundations or NGOs.

2.4 Conclusion

Sex education in this country is a very controversial issue. It is controversial for several reasons: (1) There is no public consensus on it, (2) parents often do not know what their children are learning in these classes, and (3) views and notions that have no particular relation to this subject are being promoted. *Sex education should be free of ideology; in these classes, nothing should be propagated,* but simply taught the most important things about human anatomy, conception, pregnancy and the family. Young people need to know how to protect themselves from sexually transmitted diseases, but they also need to learn about unwanted pregnancy and the health damage caused by abortion. These are scientific facts that cannot be disputed.

Sex education itself is necessary because children must be prepared for the period of puberty, and teenagers - for what sexual activity is and what it can lead to. Sex should not be talked about as something in itself - it is not only pleasure, but also a responsibility. We must educate responsible citizens, not people who think that everything is allowed to them and there are no restrictions on their freedom.

In addition to the consensus of the whole society, we must also require special training for teachers. *There should be certified teachers* who can talk to the children about this topic. But these teachers should not be specialists in fields like philosophy, sociology, journalism, etc. They must be specialists in the field of biology, medicine or psychology. We cannot allow random people to teach our children about sex!

Last but not least, it is important to control the teaching materials that are used in these classes. They should not contain shocking photos - for example, of sexual intercourse. Children can watch movies about love and family; young people can watch documentaries about venereal diseases and contraception. But all this should have one precisely formulated goal: preparation for family life.

Before concluding this chapter, we may address one objection. Maybe we should ignore sex education altogether and leave it to the parents? That is a solid argument, but there is a problem with it. Some parents do not feel ready to talk to their children about these issues. That is why they often delegate this responsibility to teachers. But there are children that learn from other children. Today, in the age of the Internet, it is even easier to access any information. We cannot prevent our kids from accessing the Internet - at least older kids can easily bypass any parental controls and go wherever they want on the internet. Therefore, this would have been possible 50 years ago. Now, this is very difficult to organize. It is right to have sex education classes in school (absolutely not in kindergarten). The only question is what their content should be. As we have shown, comprehensive education is rather encouraging education. Abstinence education, or family education, is more reliable and it will lead to a better-built society. We have to give priority to it given all our arguments formulated above.

Otherwise, in a decade we will have a society without families, without solid structure and basis. There will be only individuals freely moving like electrons. They will lack any stable worldview, they will not adhere to any moral values. Pleasure will be their only goal in life, with hedonism ruling and ruining their life.

Chapter III: Homeschooling

Education is a significant part of our lives today. From a young age, we enter the educational system - first kindergarten and then school. After that, some of us go to college as well. We hear all the time that educational degrees are important. When looking for a job, we have to say what our qualifications and diplomas are. But this is only the system of formal education. In addition to formal education, there is also non-formal education, and now we will deal with it. Speaking of the relationship between the individual and the state, we will look at this relationship in the context of education. Is there a way for parents to educate their children with the materials and methods they want?

3.1 Criticism of contemporary education system

Summary:

The modern education system has some shortcomings. Tests, grades, and educational standards make students learn things that they do not need and do not use. Here we analyze some of these shortcomings and look for a solution.

Education is a complex topic that can hardly be covered in one small chapter. Therefore, here we focus specifically on the weaknesses of the education system today in this country. Are there really any weak points to note?

We will begin by noting that probably everyone has their own ideas about reforming the education system. But such reform is difficult, and it is also challenging to achieve a public consensus. Whatever that consensus is, there will always be disgruntled parents and children. This is inevitable because it is a characteristic feature of democracy - to be able to express your opinion, even though it is different from the generally established one.

To understand more clearly why homeschooling exists today, we need to focus on the problems of the education system. Thus we will be able to make a good comparison with homeschooling as an alternative approach.

And one more note: it is essential to distinguish formal education from learning in general. We learn throughout our lives; learning is not only the acquisition of formal knowledge in a given field, but it also penetrates our experience. Our life is learning, and there is nothing striking about that. As human beings, we can learn a new fact at any moment. We never stop learning, even when we become old. Hence, learning can and does happen outside of school. We usually call such learning informal learning. Nonformal learning is learning similar to school, but not recognized by the education system. These are, for example, music, dance, sports schools, various youth trainings, etc.[2]

The problems we can note in our formal education system are the following:

1. Formalization of the educational process. Emphasis is placed on grades and test-taking.

2. Children are too passive in this process. They are rarely left to really explore anything on their own. Even when this happens, they do not do it by their will.

---

[2] We are not going too deep into the division of learning into three types. Nonformal learning stands closer to formal than to informal (experiential). Homeschooling is thus nonformal learning.

3. There is a gap between teachers and parents today. Teachers do not pay enough attention to parents, and it is not their fault. They just do not have time for it because they have too many students.

4. Education has become an expensive investment. It is very difficult for parents from poor families to meet the educational needs of their children. Textbooks, other materials, and sometimes private lessons are needed, which they cannot afford. We are not even mentioning the financial hardships associated with going to college.

5. Children do not have enough time to play and be with their friends. They do not have much time to do anything they want. In this way, we stop their potential development.

6. The modern school is strictly secularized; there is almost no place for religion in it. This reflects poorly on religious children who do not have the opportunity to stick to their faith.

Let us look at these points one by one. First, the problem with grades and testing is enormous. Our children live only with the thought of what grade they will get. Their relationships at school often depend on grades. "High achievers" are friends with other high achievers. "Low-performing students" are friends with other low-performing students. Thus, by "labeling," our children segregate themselves. This affects their self-esteem, especially the "low-performing ones."

Testing focuses on children's knowledge, but it does so in a very narrow, limited sphere. This is the state of a child's knowledge today and here. But after a few months, the same child will already have forgotten some of this information! How is it that today a child has an excellent grade in science, and a year from now the child barely remembers what the test was based on! We cannot help but think that the testing is not effective. But the problem here is different - the knowledge on which a child is tested is very broad. Children learn things that are completely unnecessary to them. Yes, if they want to, they can specialize in a field, but that should be done later.

But the testing depends on whether a student will be accepted to college, and it already depends on what career he/she will pursue! In short, our income depends on several grades that may be misplaced (there are factors that influence children's poor performance). Yes, this can be corrected later, but the label "low-performing student" remains in the mind of the child and the parents.

Pat Farenga, one of the founders of the homeschooling movement in the United States, wrote in his article from 1998: "No matter what type of education one consumes, there is no guarantee that one has actually learned it, despite tests passed and degrees earned. Adults demand that children learn facts and information that they themselves do not use or know" (Farenga 131). Tests and grades do not mean much in our lives; they were adopted only as a result of a convention. He adds that "the effectiveness of homeschooling is not measured by school test scores. Among the many reasons for this is the simple one that these tests do not cover areas outside the narrow school curriculum - areas in which homeschooled children may be learning" (Farenga 128).

On the second point, we must say that our system allows for independent experimentation. Children work on school projects. They are doing experiments in science classes. But the real problem is that they rarely have a say in what to experiment on. Usually, the teacher leads them and instructs them on what to do. Children are too passive. The real problem is that the teacher and the student are separated by a wall. This wall must be torn apart and both the teacher and student explore the world together.

The third point is rarely mentioned, and it is a symptom of the division and alienation in our society. Teachers are so busy - they really work all day, even though we do not see it. The system requires it from them. They work with so many students on a daily basis that they simply cannot even remember them well, let alone communicate with their parents. A teacher must have a group of 15 children (the same children) every day to be able to communicate with their parents easily and directly. But this is impossible today because it will affect the teacher's salary. Fewer children – lower remuneration.

The fourth point is particularly painful for poorer families in this country. Lack of good funding is a factor for early school leaving. Not to mention that it is hard to find a high-paid job without a college degree in this country. Funding opportunities are few and should be considered. The problem is that the education system itself creates this inequality. If you can pay, your child will be educated; if you cannot pay, then your child has to work and, accordingly, will not have time to study. In turn, the child will become a lower-income parent and unable to pay for his/her children's college. This is a vicious circle that needs to be broken.

The fifth point is very sad. Childhood lasts only 12-13 years. We can never be children again. Instead of playing with our friends and doing something we like; instead of spending time with our parents; instead of all that, we sit in the classroom and learn about something that does not interest us.

Of course, this is usually answered with two things: first, young children at school also learn through play; and secondly, we find our friends at school. All of this is true, but school games are different from home games. These are educational games that have specific goals. And secondly, even if we did not go to school, we would have found friends among our neighbors. Homeschooled children are just as social as other children and this is a proved fact.

The last point concerns freedom of religion and conscience. Undeniably, our education system is based on content that originates entirely from science. *Scientific theories are taught as absolutes, without alternatives, without being criticized.* Religious content in school is reduced to a minimum. Christianity is seen mostly in historical terms, in the course of world history. Believing children have no choice - they must be taught that the soul is only a "fiction," that the world began its existence with the Big Bang, that we came about as a result of chaotic evolution, etc.

This creates two problems: (1) children of believing parents are influenced by this material and become atheists, and (2) children who resist this material are ridiculed and mocked. And let us not forget the Norwegian example we gave earlier: children can even be taken away because of their parents' religiosity! In short, *the education system promotes materialism and atheism, leaving no room for people of faith.*

Here one might object: there are Catholic schools in America. Any Catholic can send their child there. This is true, but we can answer this way: Catholic schools are private and they need funding. Not every religious family can send their child there. What are poorer families to do? It is not right to kick religious children out of public schools because we are all taxpayers. The interests and needs of religious families must also be respected. Where is the respect in biology classes where they say we stand just a little bit above the apes?

Religious parents do not want all children in school to study the catechism. They do not want all children to learn about Creation. They do not want the theory of evolution to be banned. But religious children should be able to attend religious classes! In the event that a scientific theory offends their religious beliefs, they can simply skip that class and do something else instead. Let the children decide for themselves. For example, in Europe, in a number of countries, there is a subject Religion. This subject is focused on the basic principles of Christianity (in some countries, such as Greece and Poland) or compares religions (in other countries, such as the United Kingdom). If there is such a decision in Europe, why not apply it in this country as well?

Hence, modern education does have serious problems. They are not the result specifically of globalization or the emergence of the consumer society. They are contained in the very idea that the individual must obey the government. We have to pay taxes, we have to send our children to school. The problem is this coercion. Taxes are justified, but compulsory schooling is not. We should not forget that for thousands of years people have been educated at home. For example, in Ancient Greece there were no schools - at least not in the current form. Wealthier people relied on private tutors for their children. In the Middle Ages, people were educated in monasteries. Places there were limited. In the modern era, the wealthier could afford private tutors. The modern school is a phenomenon of the Enlightenment. It appeared in the 18th century and became widespread only in the 20th century.

The massification of culture, art, and here also of education lowers the level of their content. In addition, it does not allow for an individual approach. Every child needs attention. In a huge school with hundreds of students, it is impossible to pay attention to everyone. That is why there are also "dropped out" students.

What we want to pay attention to here is mainly the question of personal beliefs and convictions. In today's culture where materialism dominates and people of faith are mocked, it is difficult for a person to stick to their beliefs and values. What about a kid who most kids make fun of for going to church every Sunday or saying a prayer at school? Homeschooling is the alternative approach that allows such a child to be educated and at the same time not ridiculed at school.

Of course, modern education shows its strengths. Easy access to education allows children to learn to read and write as early as age 5. This helps them move through the school system more quickly and saves time in pursuing a hobby. Some children in Africa and Asia do not start reading until the age of 12-13, and very often, these are only boys. Quite logically, they find it harder to do because they are already behind other literate children. Poverty in Third World countries is also related to education - children work instead of studying. And they go to school with joy when they can. But we also have to admit that the most important thing for them is the knowledge they receive, not the grades. Children from developing countries are curious and have huge knowledge deficits. They want to know more about the world, but they do not have the opportunity.

It is time now to move on to the alternative approach to education that we have already talked about.

3.2 Homeschooling as the alternative

Summary:

We go on with our discussion of the principles of homeschooling. Milton Gaither explains what are the factors and causes for the emergence of this movement. Pat Farenga offers some arguments in its defense. Adam Dickerson offers his moderate criticism of John Holt's philosophy of unschooling.

Considering the weaknesses of traditional education, in the 1970s the researcher John Holt proposed reform of this system. Subsequently, he gave up his idea of reform and proposed the so-called unschooling. In practice, this new term has the same meaning as homeschooling; a term introduced later by himself. He was supported by other researchers as well as parent representatives. They believe it is right to encourage parents to educate their children at home as an alternative to traditional schooling.

First, we will turn to the researcher Milton Gaither, who describes the reasons for the emergence of this movement. In his article from 2008, he claims the most important reason is of a cultural nature: "Homeschooling... was very largely a reaction against the mass culture of the modern liberal state, a culture realized perhaps most perfectly in the consolidated public school located on metropolitan outskirts amid the rapidly expanding suburbs" (Gaither 227). This movement was accompanied (though not directly related) by the anti-segregation movement, as well as by protests against the Vietnam War. At first, it even seems left-wing in character, insofar as it is associated with the American counterculture of the 1970s.

But at the same time, a "right wing" emerged, which was driven by Christians: "The 1962 and 1963 Supreme Court decisions outlawing organized school prayer and school-sponsored Bible reading shocked and devastated many conservatives... The new rulings simply appalled many conservative Protestants" (Gaither 230-1). The secularization of the school, which we have already mentioned, turns this institution into an uncomfortable environment for a child who must be brought up in Christian values. And since there are not many existing institutions for Christian children, the educational system must be looked at differently. Why can't we educate our children ourselves? Yes, there are Catholic schools, but they are also subject to government educational standards and requirements. Therefore, homeschooling becomes a wonderful alternative to school altogether. As Gaither adds, "Although most kept their children in public schools, a growing and committed minority agreed with Christian educators such as Kenneth Gangel that 'the children of God deserve something better than pagan public education'" (Gaither 232).

We have already mentioned the reasons for this. Education today is entirely secular; it focuses on scientific theories instead of our morals and value system. We do not build personalities in school, but knowledgeable people. However, knowledge is not always related to morality. In this way, not only religious people but also people who generally have a critical view of education are oriented towards homeschooling.

The conditions in the 1970s and 1980s were suitable for a shift to the alternative approach to education. As Gaither notes, "Many conservatives lived in comfortable suburban homes that could easily accommodate a homeschool. Many housewives were well educated and committed both to their children and to staying at home" (Gaither

232). The presence of mothers at home greatly helps in the education of children in this approach; homeschooling requires the constant presence of one parent (at least until the child reaches the age of 12-13). From this point of view, this alternative approach is also not well adapted for poorer families - forced to work all day, they simply have no way to educate their children at home. However, there is a solution for this as well - for example, joint learning together with children from other families.

We should not underestimate the role of the location of the homes of people involved in this process. As Gaither reports, "homeschooling happened because of suburbanization. The suburbs' deracinated and media-saturated environs incubated the alienation that led so many young people to challenge the system by leaving it, founding communes, and pioneering homeschooling." Additionally, as he puts it, "Suburbanization facilitated segregation by race, income level, age, number of children, and cultural style, thus feeding the American hunger for privacy" (Gaither 233). Thus, children find themselves brought up together with other children who share the same values and life experiences. This reduces not only the likelihood of confrontation with other worldviews, but also of physical violence, which often occurs between children of different social backgrounds.

Therefore, in addition to cultural reasons, we can also mention social ones. The desire for children to belong to the family tradition, to the worldview professed by their parents - this is the basis of homeschooling. The school is seen and felt as something foreign. As Gaither states, "As public schools grew larger, more bureaucratic and impersonal, less responsive to parents and less adaptable to individual or local cultural variations, many families felt increasingly alienated" (Gaither 234).

Having made a brief review of the reasons for the occurrence of this phenomenon, we will now give the floor to the companion of John Holt, who has done a lot to popularize this approach. This is Pat Farenga, who, in an article from 1998, made several important observations.

According to Farenga, the personal touch is the hallmark of homeschooling. The individual approach means that the parent considers the needs, interests and capabilities of the child. Farenga writes the following: "Most homeschoolers, like the general public, feel that children will not learn anything unless it is specially taught to them. They have no qualms about the need for education; it is educational methods and content, private or public funding, that concern them instead" (Farenga 127). As mentioned, the most critical problem of the education system is assessment and testing. Children must achieve certain results, which might decide their future career. But in homeschooling there is no testing, no grades: "My wife and I are not managing child development; we are simply nurturing our children" (Farenga 128).

The last quote means that we do not need to control our children's development; we do not need to set specific goals for a child; it is a spontaneous process in which the goals at first simply do not exist. The child only directs him/herself to what the child needs. The parent can help, explain, look for educational resources. There is nothing urgent about this approach, nothing to develop within a given time frame. That is why Farenga notes that "some homeschooled children do not learn to read until they are 10 or 12; others learn at much younger ages." That is why children also have normal self-esteem - they are not "failures": "Some children who are labeled 'learning disabled' in school lose that behavior when they learn outside of conventional school, indicating that, for some, the learning environment may be more toxic to learning than are the child's genes" (Farenga 129).

Without a doubt, the school environment often inhibits learning. For example, aggression (verbal or physical) can greatly affect a child's grades. The competition between students to get the highest possible grades also results in them not learning anything. They just get high marks and then forget what they learned. Also, in class, students sometimes get distracted. They talk to each other, follow social networks, or simply ignore what is being taught. This is impossible at home - the parent can always control the discipline. And the main reason for the distraction of students is the lack of interest in the material. When the material is interesting to them, then they focus well on it.

Yes, the school should be a community. However, it is a formal community, i.e., its participants are there out of obligation. On the other hand, homeschooling can be practiced by real communities with similar views and value systems. A child does not have to sit alone at home; the child can meet other children, and study together.

This is exactly the beauty of this approach - parents can choose other families with whom to educate their children together: "Homeschooling shows us how we can view teaching and learning as a shared endeavor between families and communities, rather than as top-down managed , universal, compulsory schooling." (Farenga 132). There is no principal or managers here to monitor the learning process; no educational standards; no grades; there are no exams. There is mutual respect and trust between the "teachers" and the children. There is no strict imposition of discipline, no fear of possible exams and tests, of possible "failure."

It is usually said that the school's main task is to prepare future citizens. They must have the necessary knowledge and skills to be part of American society; protect American interests abroad; help the American economy. But homeschooling does this job no worse than formal schooling. That is why Farenga remarks the following: "Parents can seek to work with their children to help them become citizens who want to participate in the shaping and molding of their society" (Farenga 132). Therefore, homeschooling stands near the goal: to teach children to be citizens of America.

After all said, we can note the advantages of homeschooling:

1. Individual approach to the child. The parent takes into account the needs and qualities of the child. There is no massification.

2. The child learns what he/she wants. There is no compulsion. The child is motivated to learn because he/she has this desire. This is a semi-voluntary process.

3. No grades, no testing. The child does not go to school in fear of teachers and tests. He/she does not get "labeled" because of grades. His/her self-esteem does not suffer from grades or exams.

4. The child has time to sleep, play, engage in his/her hobby. Homeschooling usually takes between 30 minutes and 1 hour per day.

5. The child adheres to the values and worldview of his/her parents. He/she does not learn about things that contradict his/her worldview. This actually solves the problem of sex education, for example.

6. No bullying, no violence. Physical and psychological traumas are thus avoided. The child carefully selects his/her environment and meets new friends with similar values.

7. No need to buy expensive textbooks and resource materials. No need to think about clothing and transportation. This saves money and time.

In addition, the child can still make friends and socialize. No one prevents him/her from doing sports, playing, or going to the library. The child can attend various cultural and sporting events.

To better understand the philosophy of homeschooling, we now turn to researcher Adam Dickerson. In his book dedicated to John Holt, Dickerson describes the basic principles of this approach. Dickerson offers a moderate criticism that allows us to understand this philosophy better. He admits that the attitude toward homeschooling in academic circles is dismissive: "Holt's ideas about learning and education have had a substantial impact on the world; but despite this, those ideas have attracted very little scholarly attention. In the literature written and read by 'educational theorists'... he is barely present" (Dickerson 3). And this is precisely why homeschooling parents are mocked. The scientific community itself ignores this phenomenon, and then other people refer to this ignoring and explain that homeschooling is just a "hoax."

Holt's stance on learning is very important, according to Dickerson. There's no way a kid can learn much in school, Holt thinks. In principle, schooling and learning are opposites: "Not only is education hostile to the acquisition of the best sort of learning, it in fact tends to be damaging to the agent qua inquirer" (Dickerson 19). Although John

Dewey, the famous educational theorist, believed that the student should be a researcher, this is not applicable in school. You cannot be a researcher if you are following a predetermined plan.

Learning by doing happens outside of school. As Dickerson explains, "To learning as a by-product of genuine 'doing,' Holt opposes 'education.' As he uses this term, it involves undertaking activities which are intended as a means of producing certain learning outcomes." But these results are the problem in this case. As Dickerson puts it, "Educational activities are not intended to be worth doing for their own sakes, but for the sake of the valued future outcome that they are intended to accomplish" (Dickerson 43). Or this is what we have already mentioned - learning is not a process in itself, but there are certain goals, and students must stick to these goals. They cannot set other goals or outcomes for themselves.

However, all this does not mean that the child is the absolute center of the world. Holt is very careful in this regard, as Dickerson states: "Despite its emphasis on the freedom of the learner, Holt's position can thus be seen, in an important sense, as an inversion of a 'constructivist' and 'child-centred' approach . Knowledge is not shaped to the learner's desires and experience" (Dickerson 70). Knowledge transforms and changes the child. Or in short, Holt's position is not subjectivist; he does not claim that we can imagine things and declare them to be true. On the contrary, we must stick to the facts. But the subject of learning must be constantly active, not passive, as happens in school.

Learning is an independent process, but it still happens in the presence of other people. It does not matter if we talk about a teacher, a parent, an assistant, or a librarian. We never learn pretty alone. This principle applies specifically to nonformal learning.

This is also emphasized by Holt - the role of the community is very important. *Homeschooling does not mean social isolation of the child*; on the contrary, it should strive for more contacts.

One of Holt's books "examines how communities can build counter-institutions that 'help people do things better'—that open the world of practices to learners in ways that are compatible with their freedom and autonomy." As Dickerson adds, "The examples discussed by Holt in this book include learning exchanges, that offer free courses taught to all-comers by volunteers from the community; community libraries of various kinds of resources; community sporting associations and facilities" (Dickerson 82). It is ,therefore, incorrect to speak of the homeschooling movement as anti-social; it is rather opposed to official institutions, and above all, to the school.

Dickerson continues, noting that "the homeschooling movement was... to be the building of a counter-institution of mutual aid, in opposition to the bureaucratic, authoritarian official education system" (Dickerson 84). It is a new system where people communicate face-to-face, where children's needs and interests are taken into account rather than replaced by artificially imposed needs and demands from above.

Dickerson, at times, criticizes this movement, but in moderation. He highlights the fact that there is a serious discrepancy between the goals Holt once set and the reality today. According to him, the homeschooling movement is mostly driven by parents who isolate themselves from society because of their disagreement with certain views and practices. They are not doing enough to be a part of society and raise future good citizens of America. According to Dickerson, "homeschooling seeks to extend liberalism's 'sphere of freedom' to children's educational provision, but does not contain within itself the seeds of further mutual aid."

Then, it turns out that this movement does not oppose the instrumentalism present in our society (i.e., the principle that learning serves given ends). Homeschooling, as Dickerson puts it, is "an instance of some of that society's most negative features: the decay of the public realm, and the conception of the neoliberal individual as free from all bonds of social solidarity" (Dickerson 85).

In short, the homeschooling philosophy has been accused of excessive individualism and detachment from society. It may seem so, but theoretically this is not true: in fact, the goal of homeschooling is for the child to be able to absorb the values and worldview of his/her family and community (although Holt disagrees with this - he emphasizes active learning and action). Individualism is brought up rather in school, where there is competition between students - who will be better in a given subject or in some other field (music, sports). Homeschooling does not lead to cutthroat competition; it actually eliminates it, thus preventing the individual from focusing solely on themselves.

Researcher Susan Franzosa, in her 1984 article, mentions some more interesting ideas of Holt's. First, according to her, in America there is a tendency toward school reform and dissatisfaction with the current education system: "Until quite recently, most Americans seemed willing to retain a belief in the potential, if not actual, efficacy of public schooling, but an increasing number of parents are now choosing not to participate in any public arrangements for education" (Franzosa 228). Homeschooling, according to Franzosa, is a kind of individualism, although Holt himself rejects this. According to

Susan Franzosa, Holt claims that "the full growth of the individual is incompatible with any form of institutional control built on community consensus" (Franzosa 229).

Holt's type of individualism is "strange" since it is based on the family. That is why it is difficult to accept this criticism. It is true that in the philosophy of homeschooling there is a conflict between nature and civilization: "Holt's analyzes of education have thus tended to be meditations on what he understands as an irreconcilable conflict between the natural individual and the oppressive and corrupting effects of organized social life" (Franzosa 230). The child is understood as naturally susceptible to knowledge, as seeking knowledge; but society gives him/her ready-acquired knowledge and thus suppresses his/her inquiring nature, innate curiosity. This is Holt's conception of the child as a "noble savage."

The nature of the child can only be preserved within the family. Children lose their curiosity and desire to learn in modern school. Susan Franzosa observes that "The home, according to Holt, is the only human institution that can be genuinely concerned with the individuals' welfare" (Franzosa 236). Only there can the "teacher" feel true sympathy and love for the child: "His directive 'to teach your own' operates as a moral imperative to parents who claim to love their children. Those who choose home schooling exemplify the highest ideals of parenthood" (Franzosa 236).

Here we clearly see that there is no room for individualism in the philosophy of homeschooling. The child becomes a person that is part of a small community. Yes, this is not the whole society; yes, the child does not necessarily adhere to the worldview that the majority of citizens adhere to. But this is neither individualism, nor self-centeredness.

Gradually we move on to the critique of homeschooling. Now we will find out what exactly parents who practice this educational approach are accused of.

3.3 Criticism of homeschooling

Summary:

In what follows, we will discuss some criticism of homeschooling. According to Elisabeth Bartholet, the homeschooling movement violates children's rights, and it should be severely restricted. Some legal arguments are given pro and contra this thesis.

Not surprisingly, the harshest criticism of homeschooling comes from the liberal camp. The very idea that parents can educate their children themselves is frowned upon by our liberals. In this way, the liberal worldview, which is imposed on us from all sides, loses its impact. That is why our liberals are making every effort to limit homeschooling in this country.

Here we will refer to Elizabeth Bartholet, who, in her 2020 article, subjects homeschooling to severe criticism. According to her, homeschooling violates the human rights of children, and therefore this practice should be restricted. She makes various legal, ethical, and psychological arguments in favor of her thesis.

Bartholet begins her article with the following shocking words: "Homeschooling is a realm of near-absolute parental power. This power is inconsistent with important rights supposedly guaranteed to children under state constitutions and state legislation throughout the country" (Bartholet 3). According to her, children are oppressed by their parents. Children are endowed with the right to decide how they should be educated, and parents have no right to guide them in this sphere at all. There are many cases of child abuse that are disguised under the name of homeschooling. She gives some examples that should shock the reader so that he/she gets the wrong idea about this educational approach.

This researcher's thesis is that federal and state laws give parents too much freedom. She believes that their activities at home should be more strictly regulated. Without saying it explicitly, Bartholet probably thinks that homeschooling should be outlawed altogether. She expresses her criticism in the following passage: "Formal law, of course, does not affirmatively grant parents the right to deny education or to commit child maltreatment. But effectively it does just this by allowing homeschooling and failing to regulate it in meaningful ways" (Bartholet 3). She adds that there is a lack of regulation regarding homeschooling. Parents can do whatever they want with their children by simply filing reports with the state authorities, thus bypassing the law.

According to this author, homeschooling advocates have two main claims: factual and legal. The factual view is that home-schooled children have similar grades and results to school children. No clear difference can be found between them when it comes to applying to college and finding a job. The legal claim, she says, is based on the view that parents have the right to decide how their children are educated. It is a right belonging to the parents, not the children.

Bartholet points out that "The legal claim made in defense of the current homeschooling regime is based on a dangerous idea about parent rights—that those with enormous physical and other power over infants and children should be subject to virtually no check on that power." She adds that "That parents should have monopoly control over children's lives, development, and experience. Those parents who are committed to beliefs and values counter to those of the larger society are entitled to bring their children up in isolation" (Bartholet 6). The last words show clearly what is the reason for this attack - for Bartholet and liberals like her, parents should simply leave their children to the school that will educate them in a certain worldview and values. Parents can only deal with their value system, but they cannot control their children in any way. So, the liberal worldview dominating our school will also assimilate the children of conservative parents. This will solve the "problem" with conservatism!

Still, is Bartholet right to claim that homeschooling only expresses the notion that parents have absolute power over their children? This is not right. Parents practicing this approach do not think of their children as their slaves. They believe it is right for a child to be brought up in the spirit of family tradition, family values. A child must respect these values. Yes, the child has the right to decide whether to adhere to these values later. When he/she turns 18, for example, a child decides only what to do with his/her life. No one can isolate him/her from society! But Bartholet is afraid of something else - that children raised at home by religious parents will continue to adhere to these values. And this precisely proves the inadequacy of the liberal (pro-centralized) approach here.

However, Bartholet continues her criticism in the same direction, writing the following: "The legal claim stands in contrast with human rights treaties and with the constitutional law of most other nations. These laws recognize that children have powerful rights both to education and to protection against maltreatment" (Bartholet 7). Here we can object like this: first, homeschooling does not take away children's right to education; and second, homeschooling has nothing to do with abuse! Abuse can also occur in families with school-going children and those with homeschooled children. The two things have nothing in common.

Regarding the universal right to education - yes, children have such a right. It is written in the Convention for the Protection of the Child, as well as in the laws of a number of developed countries. But nowhere is it explicitly stated that children should only go to school. For example, in schools there are different forms of education - there is also an absentee form for children with health or other problems. There is also evening training for working students. And during the covid crisis, we saw that children can be educated from home, albeit in the online presence of teachers. During the covid crisis, many parents were at home helping their children with their studies. It was a partial form of homeschooling. The children were in total isolation from their friends and classmates, but the government did not think twice about it. Hence, the risk of abuse in such circumstances is no higher than the likelihood of homeschooling.

Bartholet herself admits that there are objective reasons why parents choose homeschooling. According to her, "Some parents choose homeschooling because they feel that their children will be discriminated against in the public schools, denied disability accommodations, or bullied. ... Some choose homeschooling... because of the flaws they see in traditional education" (Bartholet 10). Additionally, some families simply live in remote areas and their children are better off being homeschooled. There is no way that all homeschooling activities can be reduced to just one reason and one motive. Why then does she claim that the purpose of these parents is to deliberately isolate their children from other children, from educational institutions?

One of the important reasons that this researcher overlooks is freedom of religion. There are parents who consider the school to be an institution promoting atheism. Yes, the school is constitutionally supposed to be worldview neutral. But its very character as a secular institution already means that the school is not neutral. It denies Christianity, it denies the Bible, and Christian practices (e.g., prayer). The Bible is read as a historical or literary work, not as a source of Truth. Scientific theories are viewed in the context of atheism and materialism (the world is only matter and spirit is a secondary function of matter). Parents have the right to discuss these questions at home - such as where the world came from, what life is, why we are here, why there is spirit and matter, what good is, etc. When their children go to school, parents do not have enough time for this, and children often "absorb" uncritically what they are told at school.

Here, Bartholet decides to target the more extreme religious groups that she gives as an example of homeschooling. As she notes, "Members of a variety of religious groups are included today in this conservative Christian wing, including many Mormons, Jehovah's Witnesses, and Seventh-day Adventists" (Bartholet 12). These cults, she claims, aim to isolate their children from the values and culture of the majority. This is a rather radical example because the majority of homeschooling parents do not belong to these cults. One isolated example does not give an idea of the whole, of all parents that use this educational approach.

Here, this researcher continues with the legal dimensions of homeschooling. She offers examples of various court cases and decisions of the U.S. Supreme Court. According to her, "A major goal of the homeschooling movement was to establish parents' right to homeschool as a powerful constitutional right triggering strict scrutiny, making all regulation presumptively unconstitutional" (Bartholet 27). She argues that the movement has not achieved its goal because of a series of Supreme Court decisions that do not allow these parents to have absolute rights over their children (as she interprets it): "U.S. Supreme Court doctrine makes it clear that states are free to impose reasonable restrictions on homeschooling, and the state and lower federal courts have so held, interpreting both state and federal constitutions" (Bartholet 27). On the one hand, parents want a constitutional right to homeschooling; on the other hand, the courts do not allow such a right and even claim that the restrictions regarding homeschooling are justified.

Citing Wisconsin v. Yoder, 406 U.S. 205, 233 (1972), Bartholet states the following: "There, the Court held Amish parents exempt from compulsory education requirements after the eighth grade, based on parental liberty and religious freedom rights" (Bartholet 30). The homeschooling movement usually refers to this case. This case shows the moderation of the American judicial system: there should be restrictions on homeschooling, but they should not be too great. It is up to the state authorities how they will monitor what the parents are doing and how the children are progressing. But it is a fact that here the court confirms the possibility for parents to educate their children at home for religious reasons.

Bartholet is not happy with decisions like this and asserts the legislation needs to step up its pressure on the homeschooling movement. Parents, she complains, have too much freedom: "And even if the intermediate or rational relationship standards are recognized as appropriate, and courts engage in balancing conflicting interests, Supreme Court doctrine to date generally gives priority to parent—as opposed to child— rights" (Bartholet 32).

Actually, this statement is controversial. Advocates of the homeschooling movement say the opposite - that state governments impose too many restrictions on them and that it is very difficult to comply with them. For example, in some states parents must submit a study plan to the authorities; in addition, there are often home visits. This is considered unnecessary and complicating the entire process.

Bartholet goes on to say that some restrictions could even fall away under pressure from homeschoolers. As she claims, "it is unclear whether courts would generally be likely to uphold significant restrictions on homeschooling... And even less restrictive requirements, like home visits, might be struck down in some jurisdictions as overly intrusive or unnecessary" (Bartholet 37). According to her, "Movement advocates generally contend that any restrictions on homeschooling violate parental rights, even such minimal requirements as notice by parents that they are planning to homeschool" (Bartholet 49).

In Bartholet's critique, *we see the liberal camp's fear of losing control over children. Liberals wish to have the kind of control that would allow them to "promote" their views on the younger generation.* A secular school that promotes atheism and "LGBT values" is the perfect option for these people. Any child who manages to escape from such an institution is considered a "failure" of the liberal approach. Thus, it turns out that our liberals are eager to have a centralized approach and strong control by the federal authorities. And they should want the opposite - each individual should decide for himself how and what to educate himself. But this is another proof that our liberals have nothing to do with the classical liberalism of John Locke, Thomas Jefferson, Thomas

Paine. These real liberals would have never approved of such strong government control over educational institutions.

In conclusion, Bartholet claims that "We need a change in the culture surrounding child rights in general and their rights to education and protection in particular. We need a new understanding of children's constitutional and human rights, and related political and litigation campaigns" (Bartholet 58). Here we clearly see the issues we discussed in the previous two chapters—namely, whether the government "owns" our children, and whether it can impose certain content in educational programs that some parents may not agree with. The liberals believe that the government has complete power over our children with the ambition to "protect" them.

Homeschooling today irks liberals because it proves that our kids can get by away from school. And this is because learning is not identical to school. We can also learn outside of school and this is actually better learning, more effective knowledge. Our liberals are eager to hold onto a conception that binds children entirely to the curricula created by liberals. Any alternative to this is called "restriction of children's rights" as if they should be educated only outside their homes.

3.4 Conclusion

In the homeschooling situation, we again see the problem of what the children's rights are and who protects them. Who does education depend on - the parents or the government? Can the government put pressure on parents to force them to send their children to school? Should we follow the European model where homeschooling is barely allowed legally?

Homeschooling is a completely natural educational approach that has been used for centuries. It is not by chance that King Solomon also says the following: "Listen, my son, to your father's instruction and do not forsake your mother's teaching" (Prov. 1:8-9; New International Version). Our parents' words, their love, tradition are what keep our identity. They are the true school that teaches how to be good and avoid sin. Homeschooling should be given a chance and under no circumstances should it be restricted too much at the state or federal level.

We should add firmly that no educational model is absolutely right and working. Every educational system has its shortcomings. Homeschooling is not the universal solution that will make our children super smart. There are many factors influencing the effects of education: family environment, individual traits, motivation, etc. We cannot (and we are not allowed to) focus only on one approach. As we saw during the coronavirus crisis in 2020/21, we could employ a mixed approach to school (partially in class, partially at home). At any rate, we have to distinguish between learning and education. Learning lasts for life, and education lasts for a short period of time. Additionally, no one can say what the effects of education should be: to have a good citizen, a nice personality, or to possess a lot of knowledge in different spheres? Or to have skills in a specific field?

We can claim that a child should become a good citizen and good personality. We need such citizens and good people in this country, here and now. One of the ways to educate children in such a manner is their patriotic education that we can also connect

with Christianity. In the next chapter we will see how to achieve this.

Chapter IV: Patriotic and Christian education in our schools

Having addressed three very important issues related to the relationship between the government and the family, it is now time to continue our discussion with another serious topic. Talking about the influence of LGBT ideology and the principle that the government has full control over our children, we logically came to the issue of education. This sphere is the easiest way for children to be indoctrinated and controlled by the liberal elite. As we noted, homeschooling is one way to counter this centralized influence. But what to do with children that go to school and cannot be educated at home?

Here we will touch upon the problem of insufficient patriotic education in this country. What are the causes of this and what are its effects? What exactly does the term "patriotic education" mean? What is its relationship to the traditional family and to Christianity? This is what we will analyze in what follows.

4.1 Patriotic education in school

Summary:

Patriotic education in the United States has come under harsh criticism. The liberal camp aims at eliminating it entirely or replacing it with a form of education that we can call quasi-patriotic. Here we will examine the arguments of our liberals and prove the need for patriotic education.

Since the end of the Cold War, there has been a very heated debate about what our children should be learning in school. During the Cold War, it was clear that we had to emphasize the leading role of the United States as the leader of the Free World, the camp of democracy. There was no one to oppose this conception, with the exception of the events of the late 1960s.

Since the 1990s, however, the topic of patriotic education has become controversial. Suddenly it turned out that the values that made us strong for so long were "unnecessary" and even "harmful to our society." The liberal camp began to dominate significantly the media, education, and to some extent, domestic politics. The word "patriotism" turned out to be a bad word with a negative meaning. Our liberals began to criticize our 'colonial past,' our 'history of slavery'; in short, they began to instill in us a sense of guilt and of sins committed in the past. Instead of the world's leading democracy, America has turned out to be the biggest sinner in human history!

Unfortunately, this agenda eventually reached school education. Starting with Hollywood, our liberals have decided to attack our children's minds as well with these "new concepts" of our history. They focused on multiculturalism and the idea of "ethnic diversity" supposedly present in America. According to these liberals, we should feel proud that there are so many ethnicities and religions in this country. American identity, they say, is not important; it is something illusory. Only ethnic diversity is real.

Therefore, at the heart of this attack on patriotic education are multiculturalism, globalization and LGBT ideology. It is not easy to know exactly which of these principles dominates; but surely they are interrelated. Multiculturalism requires abandoning the idea of a single national identity; globalization forces us to abandon the idea of national and state borders altogether; and LGBT ideology requires us to abandon traditional values and the concept of family in general because they "get in the way" of LGBT people.

In this chapter, we will talk about the arguments for and against patriotic education. As one can easily understand, the media (including social media and networks) is dominated by liberal views on this issue. It is complicated to find scientific publications with arguments in favor of patriotic education. Such publications are rarely admitted to "authoritative scientific journals", and therefore people think that patriotic education is something unscientific, and even that it stands against science. We will examine several articles against patriotic education and try to answer them with clear and logical arguments.

First, we need to start with a definition of patriotic education. It is an education that teaches children love for the motherland, for its values and traditions. Patriotic education makes children proud and confidence in being free citizens of America. Additionally, it interprets the history of the U.S. as the leading geopolitical power in the world. This is patriotic education in the most general framework, without adding more details.

We must note that patriotic education has always existed in our schools; or at least from the 1840s when the more serious conquest of the Western territories began. Even then, our predecessors needed to realize their historical role. Over time, this education changed slightly – now it focuses more on the past than on the present. But the reason for this is clear - a young republic needed to reflect on its present and future; and now, America has gained experience and participated in the most important world events - the two world wars, as well as the Cold War. All this complements and expands our idea of this type of education.

We should add one more thing here. Patriotic education is not just about studying certain textbooks in class. It does not take place between teacher and students. It happens at school, at home, and in various other places - in the library, at a concert, and even in church. It does not always require a textbook; it is based on love for the country, and love is a feeling that cannot be expressed in words alone. There are symbols, feelings, emotions, values, in patriotic education. All this is learned and studied in real life, in our everyday life.

And last but not least, patriotic education is also upbringing. Parents have the task of teaching their children to love their country, its institutions and its values. In this way, parents and teachers together raise and educate children.

In the fall of 2020, President Trump's words led to a backlash among our liberals. Trump requested the foundation of a special commission to develop standards for patriotic education in schools. His speech then caused "outrage" in the multiculturalist and globalist camp. As we read in an article published in *Politico*, "President Donald Trump on Monday created a '1776 Commission' to promote 'patriotic education' and counter lessons that he says divide Americans on race and slavery and teach students to 'hate their own country'" (Gaudiano par. 1). Trump's order refers to the distortion of history by current liberals: " 'This radicalized view of American history lacks perspective, obscures virtues, twists motives, ignores or distorts facts, and magnifies flaws, resulting in the truth being concealed and history disfigured,' the order states" (Gaudiano par 6).

And this is a fact: our history is distorted through the lens of multiculturalism. We should feel guilty that our ancestors colonized free territories and tried to civilize the indigenous population. We should feel guilty that we got involved in both world wars. We should feel guilty for opposing the Soviet Union and its communist camp (in Korea and Vietnam). Our textbooks talk about the Indians as innocent victims of the English colonizers; there is no mention of their barbaric and brutal rituals, nor their refusal to come to terms with authority. There is a great deal of talk about slavery and racism; but it fails to mention that 200 years ago, few people in the world had as many rights as American citizens. Despite slavery, millions of immigrants from Europe, Japan, and China arrived in America. Were things really that bad back then? If our ancestors were truly evil and cruel barbarians, as our textbooks describe them, then no one would have come here.

Trump is absolutely right that we should turn to our Founding Fathers and their ideas and principles: "The commission is tasked with writing a report on the 'core principles of the American founding' and how these principles may be understood to further enjoyment of 'the blessings of liberty' and to promote our striving 'to form a more perfect Union' " (Gaudiano par. 10). Because it is the awareness of these principles that makes us better people and better citizens.

The establishment of this 1776 Commission aims at revising the teaching material and our attitude toward the past. It must counter the multiculturalist attempt to denigrate our history and blame us for something that is not really wrong. We should not feel like the heirs of Nazi Germany. Today in Germany it is accepted to study history from the perspective of Nazi atrocities. Germans are aware of the evils that their forefathers did to almost the whole world. But must we become like the Germans? What exactly have we done to be ashamed of?

Trump also emphasizes the need for appropriate funding of historical projects, for example, grants and scholarships: "The order also calls on agencies to prioritize federal resources to promote patriotic education, including the Department of State through its Fulbright scholars program" (Gaudiano par. 13). Grants to support educational projects in American history should be given to talented researchers and teachers.

The commission was indeed established, but it worked very briefly because of the end of Trump's term. It produced a report that contained essential insights into the liberal camp's distortion of our history. The commission proved that there is a very clear connection between the attempt to eliminate patriotic education and LGBT ideology, as well as the attack on the Church and the family. Of course, it can be said that the commission looks not only at our history books but at the general development of our society today, and that the latter is not its job. But history books are always written in a certain context, and this context must be examined; we cannot ignore it.

President Trump's conception of patriotic education is based on the assumption that we should love our country and its values. Let us now see why this concept does not appeal to the liberal camp - what are the arguments of this camp?

In an article for their book published in 2021, education researchers Randall Curren and Charles Dorn criticize this conception. According to them, patriotic education in the USA became more intense after 9/11. These tragic events did wake up the entire nation, but in the opinion of these researchers, they also led to radical manifestations against certain ethnicities and religions. The vast majority of Americans supported the wars against Afghanistan and Iraq in the wake of the 9/11 attacks. Any disagreement with these wars was ignored. Curren and Dorn write that when they began their study of patriotic education, "a defining feature of patriotic messaging in US schools... was its intensity in the post-9/11 era, as suppression of dissent, a vast expansion of domestic surveillance, racial profiling and persecution, torture, and a ruinous rush to war in Iraq" (Curren and Dorn 1-2).

These authors are dissatisfied with this "dominance of patriotism" in America. They believe that patriotism in America should take another form - not incitement to military intervention, but rather inculcation of democratic ideals and civic virtues. As they claim, "civic virtue is what schools should aim to cultivate, and that civic education should be organized around three components of it, namely civic intelligence, civic friendship, and civic competence" (Curren and Dorn 2). These scholars think that democratic values stand above patriotic ones.

Additionally, Curren and Dorn argue that we do not need to expand patriotic education in American schools. According to them, current patriotic education is sufficient. In addition, patriotic education has always been associated with democratic ideals: "The history reveals that patriotism has always been promoted in schools in the U.S. with the idea that it is both an inherently admirable attribute (a virtue) and an essential motivational basis for good citizenship" (Curren and Dorn 3).

The attack of these two researchers goes on with a definition of what patriotic education is. According to them, patriotism is not a virtue in itself, but is based on other values: "The defectiveness of both rationales for cultivating patriotism leads us to conclude that patriotism as such is not an acceptable aim of education. We defend civic virtue as the proper target for civic education" (Curren and Dorn 3). Civic virtues logically lead to patriotism, these scholars believe.

In their book, they also give an example of various schools that apply the "principle of justice" and in which patriotism is expressed more as civic activism. According to them, the values taught in school should be aimed at friendship and good relations between students, regardless of their race, ethnicity and religion: "The civic purposes of just school communities are best fulfilled when students have opportunities to befriend others as diverse as the civic worlds they inhabit, and experiential learning that connects peers across those worlds expands such opportunities" (Curren and Dorn 5).

Let us now look at what are the weaknesses of this position. These researchers claim that:

1. Patriotic education in the US after 9/11 is excessive and associated with the endorsement of military interventions.

2. Civic virtues are above patriotism.

3. True patriotism is respect for other people's values.

We can answer all this in the following way:

1. The tragic events of 9/11 showed that we need national unity, and that is exactly what happened. Patriotic education was revisited as an essential factor in our unification. People themselves wanted to talk more about our symbols and values. This was not imposed from outside, nor was it against the will of the majority.

2. Civic virtues are a good thing. It is very important to be active citizens, present ideas and concepts about the serious challenges present in our society. But this cannot occur without the existence of the nation! *A mass of people that are not united by national ideals remains just a group of people.* Without the state (as a political entity), there is no society; and the state rests on our sense of belonging to the Nation. This is especially true of the United States because there are many immigrants and their descendants in this country. Without this feeling, we would all feel indifferent to each other. There would be no solidarity, mutual aid and support. Without patriotism, there could not be civic virtues.

3. Respect for other people is a wonderful thing. People are different and we have to take that into account. But how can we value, for example, a religion that brutally violates human rights? How should we value people who, for example, are militant atheists and want to deprive the Church of all privileges? How should we treat people who are not tolerant of believers? That is why we say that tolerance also has its limits. Let us be tolerant of those who adhere to our values. They must obey our laws and respect our traditions. If they are not happy with that, then they can simply find a country where the lifestyle appeals to them more.

There is also a misunderstanding of patriotism as a love of war. The second is actually militarism. It is a movement and also an attitude in support of war. We have to account for the fact that anti-Islamic sentiment in this country became very intense after 9/11; it did not just appear because someone introduced it intentionally. The interventions in Afghanistan and Iraq were supported by the majority of Americans because we believed that by doing so we would reduce the risk of future attacks of this kind. Ultimately, these interventions were unsuccessful insofar as they did not introduce democracy to these countries. But that now depends on the local citizens, not on us. We should also add that our withdrawal from Afghanistan directly returned the Taliban to power, which only shows that this withdrawal was unnecessary.

In his 2006 article, the researcher Joel Westheimer criticized the same patriotic urge that spread after 9/11. According to him, patriotic education in America is the result of political interference and "psychological manipulation." He criticized the role of politics in education. As he reports, "On 12 October 2001, the White House, in collaboration with the politically conservative private group Celebration U.S.A., called on the nation's 52 million schoolchildren to take part in a mass recitation of the Pledge of Allegiance" (Westheimer 609). Congress also passed a Resolution requiring students to recite this.

Westheimer believes that this interest in patriotic education is forced, that it is external to children. Politicians, legislators, media and even teachers participate in this enforcement. He notes that "Many teachers and administrators have implemented mandatory policies, shunned controversy, and reinforced the America-is-righteous-in-her-cause message, just as the Bush Administration and politically conservative commentators have wanted" (Westheimer 609). In doing so, he blames the Bush administration itself for this "forceful imposition."

Nonetheless, this author continues by saying that the attacks of 9/11 also provoked a debate about difference, otherness. What should be our attitude toward Islam, for example? Westheimer points out that "terrorism, war, and the threat of fundamentalist intolerance have sparked other educators' commitments to teaching for democratic citizenship, the kind of citizenship that recognizes ambiguity and conflict" (Westheimer 609). In short, he believes that after this tragedy there is a debate between two sides - the patriotic side and the side that stands on the side of "tolerance."

According to Westheimer, in fact, patriotism in itself can be divided into two types: authoritarian (focusing only on the positive image of the Fatherland; does not allow disagreement) and democratic (focusing on friendship and tolerance, allows for a critical stance) (Westheimer 610). The first kind of patriotism imposes specific standards of national identity and forcibly urges all citizens to aspire to them. This is an "intolerant" patriotism that does not recognize foreign opinion and opposition. It puts our nation above all others in the world. The other kind of patriotism, according to Westheimer, recognizes the existence of different ethnicities and religions; it is tolerant and based on the idea of pluralism. Everyone has the right to adhere to their value system. All nations are seen as equal. As he describes the second type of patriotism, "Caring about the substantive values that underlie American democracy is the hallmark of democratic patriotism. This does not mean that democratic patriots leave no room for symbolic displays of support and solidarity" (Westheimer 612).

Surely this opposition is manipulation. The second kind of patriotism is a false, utopian ideal that cannot be realized. The first kind of patriotism is just a caricature. This author definitely confuses patriotism with militarism, with the desire for war. After all, the idea that our nation stands above others should not be taken literally; we are not 'superheroes,' nor are we a 'superior race.' Nazism is only a distortion of the concept of love of country. We think of America as standing above other nations for two reasons:

first, this is a fact today (in an economic and geopolitical sense); and second, it is because

of our love for our country. We do not want to prove that America is number 1 for us

constantly; there is no need for that. But the fact is: our nation is the strongest in the

world, and everyone else conforms to it. If it were not, there would not be so many

applicants for immigration in this country!

There is one more thing to say here. Patriotism is a completely moral thing

because *the most natural thing in this life is to love your country and your family.*

Patriotism is based on this love for the land, for the traditions and the ancestors.

Patriotism does not create borders because they have existed for many centuries; it guards

the boundaries within which a given community of people (family, clan, entire city, etc.)

lives. The us-them divide is very real, and it was not created by President Trump or any

conservative in the 19th century. Likewise, we can argue that this division does not

automatically lead to hatred of "others." Why should we hate other nations of the world?

But we can set a moral standard to guide them. And when they do not meet that standard,

we have the right to point the finger and criticize them. Is there anything wrong with

that?

Hate is not the basis of patriotism. We should not be xenophobic, but the liberals

blame us for this very thing! Here they create a straw man argument - they put words in

our mouths that we did not say. The examples with the Nazis, as well as with the slave

owners of the 19th century, are not appropriate - today we live in a different world, in a

world of globalization and merciless removal of borders. *Patriotism today is precisely a*

reaction against this attempt to erase our national memory and our traditions by the

globalists.

The Republican administration (the article was written during Bush's time) is strongly criticized by Westheimer. According to him, the patriotic atmosphere created at the beginning of the 21st century is incorrect and inadequate. There is no single American credo, as many patriots believe: "Sen. Alexander and like-minded politicians suggest that Americans, despite diverse backgrounds and cultures, all share a unified American creed or a common set of beliefs and that these beliefs are easily identifiable" (Westheimer 615). Moreover, patriots believe in the justice of any American intervention in the world: "The events of the Iraq War and the ongoing 'reconstruction' have led policy makers and educators who favor authoritarian patriotism to prefer celebrating what President Bush has repeatedly called 'the rightness of our cause'" (Westheimer 616).

Here we see clearly that, according to Westheimer, this patriotism is deliberately imposed in order to justify various military interventions. But it is not clear by whom it is imposed. After all, American citizens themselves - especially the parents of school students - spread the patriotic practices described above. In some cases, students themselves want to recite patriotic poetry and honor our national symbols. It is incorrect to claim that President Bush "created" this patriotic atmosphere. Also, this spontaneous surge of patriotism was a response to the terrorist threat that effectively put America at war for the first time since 1945. The terrorists wanted to see a scared America, but instead, they did the opposite - they managed to unite the American people into one, despite all the ethnic and religious differences. This, we repeat, was a spontaneous process that was neither artificially imposed nor forced.

According to Westheimer, however, unification is not necessary. He thinks that absolute agreement is not what we should aim for. The ideals of "democratic patriotism" require pluralism, dissent, criticism. He notes the following: "Trying to forge a national consensus in any other way or on any other grounds... is what leads to troubled waters. And students need to learn about these contentious debates with which adults struggle and prepare to take up their parts in them" (Westheimer 620). This is not an illogical position: since ancient Greece, we have known that truth is born in the dispute, in the discussion. It is good to have different perspectives on a problem. But it is not true that we can live without consent; every society needs stability, and this is not achieved through arguments and discussions.

Some liberals embrace the "American way" in sense of egocentrism and individualism; they think that we should live forever for ourselves, with our own values and views. But this is not the case: a just and stable society must have agreement on its goals, ideals and values. No society can survive without unity (to some extent). We do not need to have complete unity - someone can always criticize the majority's point of view. But absolute pluralism is not a good option here either - it will lead to greater division, which our external enemies - especially Russia and China - will benefit from.

"Democratic patriotism" is based on the principle that all citizens in a society should live well. Westheimer claims that "To be a democratic patriot, then, one must be committed not only to the nation, its symbols, and its political leaders, but also to each of its citizens and their welfare" (Westheimer 612). We may agree with this statement: a true patriot should care for the welfare of all other fellow citizens. The nation is not just an abstract idea; it consists of specific individuals with specific needs. But this prosperity cannot be achieved either by accentuating disagreement and differences. We cannot allow the existence of parallel value systems that do not respect human rights or place religious fanaticism on a pedestal. We cannot allow the existence of various cults that can abuse their members, and this is happening against our laws.

Wsettheimer's critique is wrong because it starts from a false premise: that patriotism can be divided into types. Patriotism is only one. A person that defends globalism cannot be considered a patriot; there is no way a person that thinks all value systems are the same can be a patriot. Moreover, patriotism is not incompatible with democracy. Patriotism is love for the homeland, for the nation. A stable state must be democratic; tyranny and authoritarian rule are not identical with patriotism.

In a 2021 article, researcher Thor Reimann denies the need for special patriotic education. According to him, the most important thing is the welfare of the people, not whether they adhere to traditional values and patriotism. He refers to a specific case - The governor of Texas signed a bill regarding patriotic education. Reimann describes the content of this bill as follows: "These pamphlets must contain information highlighting Texan values and iconic Texan histories, like the Texas War for Independence, Juneteenth, the indigenous people of the Texas land" (Reimann par. 1).

This author thinks that our patriotism is based on injustice and inequality - this is already a well-known thesis. As he notes, "While 'patriotic education' claims to highlight our nation's bedrock values and commemorate American progress, it runs the risk of celebrating unfulfilled accomplishments and undermining ongoing injustice." As he goes on, "Artificially injecting patriotism into our education system is therefore dangerous and has the potential to be inaccurate" (Reimann par. 3).

But why does this have to happen artificially? We have already mentioned that enthusiasm for our past and values is not something imposed by external forces. Our people, our society, want this themselves. The truth is that liberals want to push a certain agenda and see the same in the efforts of the other camp.

The following is an unsound comparison between our patriotism and what is called that in Communist China. According to Reimann, "Patriotic education programs are indeed used in other parts of the world, but they definitely aren't parts of the world that Republicans like Abbott would want to emulate; China, for one" (Reimann par. 4). But here we must say that the author has not read Marx, Lenin and Mao well. The basis of communism is the idea of a class revolution of the workers; no matter their nationality or ethnic origin. All workers have one motherland - communism, as the ideologues of communism believe. The fact that in China or the USSR they call a certain doctrine "patriotism" does not mean that it has anything to do with it. In addition, there are many different ethnicities in China, and dozens of different languages exist there. It is very difficult to unite all these ethnicities under the general label "Chinese nation." China is a country, but not a nation.

This vain attempt to compare American patriotism with the pseudo-patriotism of the Chinese only shows that our liberals have no good arguments. In general, the whole article is full of various thoughts of the author, who does not try to prove them. He wants to counter those he makes up himself. For example, according to him, conservatives claim that almost all U.S. universities are left-wing, as are many teachers. In fact, there are no such claims - this is an exaggeration. It is clear that there are teachers with different political views. But according to Reimann, "And while statements that teachers tend to lean liberal do have merit, the idea that schools are pushing leftist ideology through their curricula does not. In truth, schools have frequently accommodated right-leaning concerns" (Reimann par. 10).

Here this author mixes different ideas and theses. In all this chaotic material, we can only see some defense against vague criticism from conservatives. But he also goes on a counter-attack: in fact, the school has a rather right-wing agenda! Yes, he is referring to the patriotic wave that swept through our country after 9/11. But again, he does not prove anything, he just throws around random statements.

Reimann expresses his fear that conservatives have an increasing influence on society: "Patriotic education campaigns aren't just taking hold in Texas, though — they're seeping across the country. Many states, in largely Republican-led efforts, are attempting to legislate the way we talk about race and identity in the classroom" (Reimann par. 6).

But this author does not say what is the reason for these legislative attempts. Does this whole process just happen for no reason? We have already mentioned that in our history books some of our heroes are seen as "racists"; too much emphasis is placed on slavery; guilt oozes from every page of these textbooks. But it is not just that; our very history as a nation is threatened by a new narrative - one that claims we are colonizers, conquerors, invaders! We all know that the truth is exactly the opposite - America was created by free people who escaped from oppressive regimes in Old Europe. America was created by immigrants who were looking for their piece of land to rebuild their lives. America was made by both Protestants and Catholics, Jews and Buddhists; why did they come to this particular country and not somewhere else? Why didn't they stay in their countries? Because when America had a constitution and legal protection of human rights, in England, France, Germany, Austria, Spain, there were only regimes and violation of these rights. Because while our ancestors were building homes and developing their lands, the European powers were at war with each other (mostly Germany, Austria and France). Our ancestry comes from these freedom-seeking immigrants; and yes, when we insist that these immigrants were Americans, we do not automatically become xenophobes. They were not colonizers, they did not come with the aim of enslaving other people.

It is true that relations with the indigenous population (Indians) were very complicated and difficult. It is true that they lost lands, but that is because most of them did not seek reconciliation with our ancestors. Most natives were civilizationally backward, which is why our ancestors tried to integrate them. This was quite possible, but the natives refused.

If our ancestors at that time had decided to go back to their countries (England, Germany, etc.), America would not have existed today. Perhaps the indigenous people of North America would have lived here, but at what cost? Once upon a time, these people had to become civilized; they would seek a treaty with the immigrants from Europe. But the United States would not have existed today then, and no one knows what the history of mankind would have been. What would have happened during the two world wars if our ancestors had only lived in Europe? Maybe Europe would have been dominated by a nationalist Germany today (still, this is only speculation).

America is the land of hope, opportunity, optimism, and dreams. It is part of our history and identity. There is no way you can tell our young children that our ancestors were colonizers. First, this is not true, only a few of them were; and secondly, it is a moral judgment that should not be allowed in a history class. History consists of facts, not judgments and moral reasoning. The facts in our textbooks are replaced by estimates and even arbitrary interpretations of various events. There is a lack of information about the immoral habits and traditions of the indigenous people, which would horrify any sane person today.

Regarding slavery, there is no doubt that it was a terrible and sad thing. It is part of the history of the whole world. Every great power passed through this stage. But we have already apologized many times to African Americans. They have their place in our history and we show it regularly. But we cannot all be made to feel guilty today. We are not to blame for the slavery that existed 160 years ago. Such was life then; it is another historical and social context. Today, African Americans have all the rights and are fully equal before the law to other American citizens. There is no country in the world where they have so many rights and freedoms.

Reimann does not mention all these facts. He is not talking about our history being interpreted for political purposes by liberals. They actually serve the interests of globalists who want to eliminate all borders as well as erase the national identity of all nations. A global world without borders, ruled by a certain economic and political elite - this is their goal.

This author clearly defends the current state of our education system, because he declares the following: "The status quo of the American education system is not leftist. It is not anti-American, or anti-white, or anti-democracy. Rather, it is favorable to our history. It is celebratory of the Constitution and appreciative of the progress that we have made" (Reimann par. 11).

But is this really the case? According to many critics of the liberal narrative about our history, liberals place too much emphasis on the guilt of our ancestors. Instead, however, they make no mention at all of the barbaric practices that existed in our lands prior to the 17th century; they do not mention Spanish atrocities in South America and Portuguese atrocities in Africa and Asia. Yes, that is the problem with our liberals: they do not measure up. According to them, only America is to blame for all the evils in the world. And the fact that England, France, Germany had terrible and tyrannical regimes only 200 years ago - this does not affect them.

Critical thinking is considered something of a panacea by our liberals. According to them, when our children learn to think critically, they will no longer be patriotic. Thinking critically, they will no longer see heroes in our history. Although he does not say it directly, Reimann states something like this: "The role of our education system is to teach students to dive into and think critically about the problems that society faces. This will not happen if the state is pushing a heroized version of its history." But that is not all: "We should not have to teach patriotism. It should be a byproduct of a successful, just and equitable country. If we must teach national pride, it implies that we are living in a nation where that pride may not occur organically" (Reimann par. 14). In a word, true patriotism is to live well. But what would happen if we never lived well? Would we stop being Americans and become, say, Germans or Japanese? Or the Chinese?

This line of reasoning is full of logical and factual errors. In their quest to prevent "outside pressure" on our schools, liberals are doing just that - putting pressure on, and much more intense pressure. They throw a lot of financial resources into fighting patriotism in all spheres. They ridicule patriotism, mock our heroes and all our ancestors.

Hollywood, the media, and our universities are thrown into this battle, which is essentially being waged against America. Because America's greatest enemy is herself; more precisely, her enemies are found within her. They are working wonderfully for the benefit of Russia and China, although they do not yet realize it.

Patriotic education today is not only necessary but also vitally important for us. This is a time when many people are questioning their national identity; many people think they are believers but are actually atheists; many people believe that there are different moral systems that are equal to each other. The young generation has already grown up thinking that borders are superfluous and that they are citizens of the whole world.

But tomorrow, in such a borderless world, strong nation-states will dominate; these will be nations with a clearly expressed national identity; peoples who stick to their traditions. These nations will impose new borders on the world, and this process will not be pleasant for us at all! Liberals are pushing us right into a world where America will have no say. But then dominant forces will emerge that will completely deny the basic ideas of our liberals. And then, who will save them from these new enemies?

The truth is that we should not lose the supports we have had so far. We should not destroy the supporting pillars of our home just because we think we will be able to build new ones. In addition, today we are facing more challenges that did not exist just 20 years ago. Who would have imagined then that we would almost come to a direct confrontation with Russia (over Ukraine) and China (over Taiwan)? The views of our liberals stem from the belief that the Cold War is over forever. But today we already understand that this is not so - the Cold War never ended; it just went through a temporary truce. This means that we must go back to the principles that protected us in that difficult period and allowed us to win the Cold War. One of these principles is conveyed by the motto 'In God we trust,' and it did not appear without reason.

4.2 Christian education in marginalization

Summary:

Christian education in this country is marginalized. The attitude toward it is negative. Religion is almost absent from the curriculum, and where there is religious content, it is only in a historical context. All this comes from the wrong conception that only science gives us knowledge about the world. In fact, the highest form of knowledge is found in the Bible.

Without a doubt, the main point of attack of the new (left) liberals is Christianity. Their attack began as early as the 1970s with the legalization of abortion and the attempt to legalize practices such as euthanasia and in vitro procedures. Besides, patriotism has become the object of their criticism in the last two decades.

Of course, this is part of the secularization process that has been going on for at least three centuries. Modern times have brought with them the belief that man is the center of the world and that he alone controls his destiny. Everything exists because of and thanks to man; our concepts of truth and good depend solely on man, and they would not have existed without him.

Secularization is, first of all, a cultural process, and second, a political process. It results in the dominance of secular culture. In political terms, *secularization means separating the state from the church.* All state institutions are thus isolated from the church, and more generally, from Christianity itself. This includes the school - it becomes a place for teaching scientific theories meanwhile completely ignoring the Christian worldview.

We will not consider this issue in depth here. Our task is to show that the marginalization of Christian education is the result of the policy of strong centralization and the conception that "the child belongs to the government." In the same way that the government can safely take away children and impose its understanding of sex education on us, it can also eliminate Christianity from our schools.

What is the current situation: there is no Christian education in the public schools; prayers are forbidden; religious images are prohibited. In the textbooks, Christianity is present only historically and culturally - as a religion that once dominated our culture, but no longer does. Where scientific theories collide with Christian concepts, the former take absolute priority. This refers to questions such as the immortality of the soul, the origin of the world, and the emergence of life.

Of course, there are also Christian schools and colleges but this is a different case. With them, the teaching of Christian doctrines is allowed. But not every believing parent can send their child to such a school. Not everyone can afford it financially. The question is this: since America was founded by Christian immigrants, and Christian culture is part of our identity, why then is Christianity so severely marginalized in our schools?

First we will begin our analysis with some passages from the Bible that show the need for people to have knowledge of God. We will then analyze the arguments for and against Christian education in schools. *The Bible demonstrates quite clearly that our worldly knowledge is not enough and that we need something more - knowledge of the spirit and of Our Creator.*

In 2 Timothy we find a passage that confirms the belief that the Bible is the absolute truth and we must follow it unyieldingly:

> All Scripture is God-breathed and is
>
> useful for teaching, rebuking, correcting
>
> and training in righteousness,
>
> so that the man of God may be
>
> thoroughly equipped for every good
>
> work. (2 Tim. 3:16-17)

The Bible stands at the foundation of life itself. It is a manifestation of Truth; it contains not only knowledge of the world but also of Being itself. In the Bible everything is given to us ready and at once; there is no need to add or take anything away. It contains knowledge that has been verified by different people over the centuries. It is also the basis of our traditions, and we must constantly turn to it for advice and comfort.

In another place, we read what was written by St. Paul, and it is the following:

> For everything that was written in the

past was written to teach us, so that

through endurance and the

encouragement of the Scriptures we

might have hope. (Rom. 15:4)

We have already said that the understanding of education includes various elements and activities. Our understanding of education today is strictly limited to the school, and this should not be the case. Education should touch all aspects of life, including the understanding of the meaning of life. Why do we live? Who created us? Is there life after death? Does it have a soul? These are questions that science alone cannot answer. That is why we say that education should be much broader and not focus on scientific theories.

On the other hand, the Bible gives us faith and hope. In a world full of sin and death, we have to rely on something. We cannot merely think that life ends with physical death. It is a kind of nihilism that sees nothing permanent, nothing eternal in the world.

The problem today is that we only trust science and scientists. In fact, they cannot know everything about the world! They describe only one part of the world - the material, the physical part. As St. Paul writes, we should not consider ourselves too smart and knowledgeable:

Do not deceive yourselves. If any one

of you thinks he is wise by the standards

of this age, he should become a "fool"

so that he may become wise.

For the wisdom of this world is

foolishness in God's sight. (1 Cor. 3:18-19)

Yes, it seems paradoxical - we have to become "fools" to get closer to God. But this word here means that we should not be haughty and proud of our knowledge. Our "foolishness" is that we follow the covenants of God and we respect His Scripture. Yes, we are "stupid" for scientists, for those who believe only in science. But our "stupidity" contains much more knowledge than the greatest scientists have about the world and life. We know all about life and death, about good and evil, justice and beauty! Let them call us "fools"; it should not make us concerned.

In the book of Ecclesiastes, we find many passages concerning wisdom and knowledge. We know his pessimistic position about knowledge - he who accumulates knowledge accumulates sorrow. But the truth is that according to Ecclesiastes, we must follow the ancient tradition set before us by our Creator. We should follow the words of our wisemen and should not add anything superfluous to these words:

The words of the wise are like goads,

their collected sayings like firmly

embedded nails-given by one Shepherd.

Be warned, my son, of anything in

addition to them. Of making many books

there is no end, and much study wearies

the body. (Eccl. 12:11-12)

Yes, there is no use in reading too many books, too much knowledge. This may sound strange, but it can be explained like this: when we read book after book, we begin to think that we know everything. We become conceited and even arrogant in our pride. There is something else: knowledge and wisdom are different things. Wisdom is concerned with how to live virtuously and rightly. Knowledge describes the world as such, without reference to our personal lives. Cold knowledge, if we can call it that, has nothing to do with morality. It simply describes the world; but it is a great mistake to think that it is sufficient. We must know how to live, and this has been repeated by all philosophers since Socrates. We have no use for such cold knowledge that leaves us without any instruction as to the meaning of life.

What does all this mean for Christian education in schools? We must perceive education in another sense - as learning how to live; this is a principle introduced as far back as Ancient Greece. The Christian worldview is the only worldview so far that has withstood all the tests of time, all social, cultural and economic changes. It helps us navigate the world, find meaning in our lives, and believe and hope in immortality. Christianity teaches us that matter is not the "mother" of spirit; on the contrary, spirit once created matter. Christianity teaches us that life did not arise by chance from a strange interaction between material entities but was created completely purposefully and with some design by a Great Creator. Last but not least, Christianity teaches that the Good as a moral category is absolute, it is not a relative and subjective thing. In school, our children rarely learn about the good; yes, good deeds and education are spoken to them; but this is not enough. How do you explain to children that goodness makes sense in a world governed by chance, a world in which unjust actions are not punished by a higher authority?

Our liberals answer like this: goodness is not learned in school but in life. Not every atheist is a bad person, they say. Religion does not always teach us good, these liberals add.

This is a very old argument used since the Renaissance. Morality and religion, these people say, are different things. They cannot explain the fact that the first ethical rules written down on paper were precisely related to religion. Our Decalogue undoubtedly marks the beginning of the written formulation of morality. But by their very actions, these liberals are contradicting themselves. Since they believe so much in morality, why then declare it subjective? Why do they think that each person should adhere to their own value system? Likewise, they also state that a person belongs to the gender to which they feel they belong. In general, this is a philosophy of the subjective - there is nothing that is real and objective, regardless of my perceptions and understandings. Where is this morality these liberals talk about?

Another argument they make is that all religions are equal and constitutionally we cannot give preference to Christianity. To this, we can answer as follows: any child may wish to attend certain religious education classes. Three or four hours per week can be allocated for such a visit. We will not require Muslims to attend Catholic catechism classes. But we cannot stop believing students from participating in such classes. And the situation at the moment is exactly like this - there is such a ban, which stems from a misunderstanding of the First Amendment (no official religion established in the United States).

In line with the previous chapters that we have analyzed here, we can say that this is a tendentious marginalization of Christianity. The idea is that children are separated from their families and raised in atheistic values that teach them that pleasure is our only purpose in life, and that our goal in life is to collect commodities. This is the philosophy of hedonism and consumerism. It fits perfectly into the agenda of the globalists, for whom children should have no permanent, stable values; they only need to buy so that the economic elites can accumulate profits.

Eliminating patriotism and Christianity from our schools will send us into a globalist spiral. We will be constantly moving and thinking that we are evolving; but in fact this development will be external, foreign to us. As we have already mentioned, the time will come when we will find out the hard way that every nation must adhere to stable and permanent values.

Finally, one might argue: should we rely on school to educate our children in Christian values? Should not this be happening at home? Why should teachers be involved in the education of children?

All of this is true. We should not rely entirely on the school to educate our children. Family is most important in terms of education. But the problem is that the government wants to take control of the very upbringing of our children. This is done in various ways, as we have already noted in this book. This should not be allowed - if we surrender now and leave everything in the hands of the liberal camp, it will come forward and demand more from us. Maybe they will ask us to ban baptizing our children? Maybe children under 12 will be banned from church? No one knows what may happen in the future, but this trend is alarming. The line between government institutions and the family must be sharply drawn and always reminded that it exists.

4.3 Conclusion

The government is increasingly encroaching on family territory. Parents have less rights than a few decades ago. Religious communities are under pressure today. They must reckon not simply with secularization or the separation of church and state, but with the jeers and sneers of the liberal camp. People of faith were the majority throughout Western civilization for centuries. Today they are decreasing, which is also a result of the strong pressure on the church. Freedom of religion is limited today. These days, religion has almost no importance in our lives, except in the narrow family circle.

With patriotism it is a little different. It is still difficult for it to be marginalized to such an extent. Threats from Russia, China and Islamic fundamentalism are preventing the liberal camp from eliminating patriotism from our society. However, liberals seek to "cleanse" our schools of patriotism and replace it with cosmopolitanism, i.e., the attitude that "we are all citizens of the world."

The reasons for this onslaught are difficult to specify. Probably this is due to the desire of some globalists to make the flows of capital easier. No borders, no restrictions- you can use manpower anywhere in the world, and if possible, with minimum taxes. American companies should move to Asia or Eastern Europe to increase profits. As we see, economy is thus interwoven with politics and culture. The conception of borders removal leads logically to the elimination of patriotism from schools and from society as a whole. Traditions and family values are not important anymore; we need a consumer society, and the entire world should be transformed into such, some liberals think.

Apart from the school, the media has also been used for this double onslaught. The media is yet another tool to influence our children, and one that is almost impossible to eliminate. Let us see what it is all about now.

Chapter V: The media and our children

The problem of the media needs comprehensive analysis. Here we will work on what should be the role of the government and state authorities in relation to the media. We will conduct this analysis entirely within the context of the problem of the relationship between the family and the government.

So far, we have talked about the state demanding too much from parents. Conceptions are imposed that are not particularly popular and acceptable. Parents' freedom is limited. Nurturing and education are placed entirely in the hands of external institutions instead of parents. At the same time, exactly where the government should impose restrictions, it does not. This applies precisely to the media: both traditional media and new media.

Before we begin our analysis, we must counter an objection. We will here insist that the activities of the media should be seriously restricted in the name of public interest. But a reader will say this: you want more freedom for parents and for the family. You are against centralized intervention in family affairs. Why, then, do you want the government to step in to restrict media freedom?

This reader should see the overall context of the present work. We are talking about the fatal influence of various external factors on the lives of our children. There are clear and planned attempts to influence the thinking of our children. They should learn to be atheists, ridicule patriotism, calmly accept LGBT ideology and even to be ready to stand against their parents if someone asks them to. The media today is dominated by the liberal camp, similarly to academic institutions. National television networks are generally liberal-leaning. But today we will talk not so much about the media as a whole, but about children's content in them.

Thus, television today remains a major tool for influencing people's minds. Although many people say, "I do not watch TV" or "I do not have a TV at home," they still have access to TV content. This is not difficult today - it is enough to simply follow different TV streams even on Facebook. There is also VOD technology through which a viewer can watch whatever they want. Therefore, we follow the news whether we want or not.

Of course, we should not underestimate the new media, or what we call social networks. They also disseminate information, but the way this is done is very reminiscent of the operation of TV channels. A professional team prepares the type of material that is then distributed. The only significant difference compared to traditional television is that there the method of distribution is very limited - you must have a TV receiver and possibly a subscription. Easier access to TV content leads to increased audience.

The indisputable advantage of new media is the fragmentation of their content. Certain media platforms (or even Facebook pages) focus on certain topics. Interest groups appear. This stands in stark contrast to traditional TV channels, where more general information is broadcast and content is usually spread over hourly slots.

But the new media has one huge drawback. It is difficult to enforce control over their content. In this way, inappropriate content is directed at our children without us being able to react quickly.

Here we will talk more about traditional television because it still dominates our media world. But along with it, we will also criticize the model of the new media, which focuses only on viewers and not on the quality of its materials. But the liberal agenda can be seen in both types of media.

Television used to be a window to the world. It helped us acquire important and new information. We were able to see how people live in different countries and at different times; we were able to watch various important events live. Today, television has become a means of political control. Biased and subjective producers and journalists prepare news and TV shows that reflect their point of view. By manipulating public opinion, they introduce views that only 30 years ago were considered unacceptable or controversial.

But is it true that people working for TV are biased? Can we prove this, or is it just a conspiracy theory?

Here we will talk about the TV shows rather than the news. It is clear that the news makers are biased. This is quite normal - news should be delivered quickly and efficiently. There is no way for news editors to take in huge streams of information and process it objectively. We are more interested in what is happening in our city, our state, not in Southeast Asia. In addition, televisions pay attention to the scandalous, to the controversial, to what will attract more attention. There is no objectivity in this.

We need to add one more thing. The media is called that because it is a medium. They are not the original source of information, they only convey it. At both ends of this chain are the primary source (or the event itself and its perpetrators) and the audience (at the other end). The media aims to convey information about a given event to a given audience. This occurs in a fast and efficient way, in order not to waste time and resources. But we should not think that the media has absolute power and authority; at the other end of this chain stand the viewers, readers or the general audience of this media. We can and must exercise our power to weed out incorrect information; we have every right to criticize a given media. A society educated well in media literacy must be able to distinguish true from false information.

All this means that the problem is not the very existence of television. It is not a "devil's work" as some of its critics would claim. Television was not created to control public opinion; this purpose appeared later (first during the Russian Revolution and then during World War II). Even if we ban television (as the Taliban did in Afghanistan), we cannot completely eradicate the media. Perhaps this is possible in a closed society like that run by the Taliban; but a strong economy cannot afford it. We need to have fast and reliable access to information. We cannot talk about banning the media at all.

But what is the attitude of the media toward children, and more precisely, of children toward the media? We can safely say that *children very easily assimilate what they see, hear and read.* Young children observe the world around them; they copy the behavior of their parents or their friends. Likewise, they tend to copy various TV characters. This is optional; usually some kids are more likely to imitate TV images than other kids. This depends on the amount of time they watch TV and parental controls. But it is undeniable that children perceive the world of TV as real; for them all these characters and events are quite real. They are convinced that all these superheroes exist; likewise, they also believe in the veracity of the fairytales their parents read them. Therefore, children are a very easy "target" of the media - they easily and quickly "absorb" the information provided, without having the opportunity to think about it critically.

We cannot teach our children to think critically. Their psyche is such that they perceive the world in a naive-idealized way. It is for this reason that we must control the content they have access to; we as parents must be able to explain to our children why they cannot watch a certain TV show and why the behavior of a certain TV character is not good and moral. In this sense, parents should learn media literacy and critical thinking about media content.

The aims of TV channels related to children are clear: advertise products and services that children will want to buy. In our commercialized world, the most important thing is that the audience becomes a group of consumers who buy what is offered to them. Therefore, in this country too, there is a strong restriction on the possibility of advertising in children's TV shows. This restriction affects the products that can be advertised.

Advertising itself is not a bad thing either. In the past, advertisements directed people to certain products. The problem is that over time the ads become more and more aggressive. In order to beat their competition, certain companies provide false information about their products. There is a familiar story with the tobacco industry in the 1960s when large companies paid certain medical professionals and laboratory researchers to prove that there was no link between cancer and nicotine.

Advertising unhealthy products is also something that should not happen. It was not long ago when alcohol was often advertised on TV. Today, ads are more sophisticated, more delicate because of federal control. But companies are now advertising in new media where there is less control. In addition, there are also new ways of advertising - for example, advertising campaigns that at first glance do not look like ads at all.

However, advertising aimed at children is not the biggest problem facing our society. *The real problem we need to pay serious attention to is the hidden message contained in children's TV material.* And such hidden messages can have a huge impact on our children's behavior and thinking.

Television products are made in such a way that very often a message can be hidden. It does not need to be spoken by any TV character explicitly. It can be embodied in a given character or in a certain action. The journalist S. Atkinson gives examples of cartoons in which there is a hidden agenda. In fact, he sides with the liberal camp here, and he welcomes the presence of such hidden messages. As he states in his 2019 article, "More often than not, this is education via stealth. The best of the examples listed below don't make a big deal about taking a liberal stance on issues of identity or try and bully kids into thinking a certain way" (Atkinson).

He means here that there is no violence applied at children to learn something that someone else wants them to learn. But the fact that we are talking about invisible education is very confusing. Atkinson adds the following shocking paragraph: "They act as imaginative spaces where it goes without question that you can love anyone you want, no matter their gender" (Atkinson).

Here we see a liberal quite openly stating that there is an agenda in our cartoons! Yes, they do not offer direct messages like "You can love whoever you want." These messages are hidden – usually, they are not the focus of the episode itself. One such case can be found in the series 'Star vs. the Forces of Evil' (tv series from 2015-2019).

Against the background of music, viewers see several kissing couples during a concert - man and woman, man and man, woman and woman. Atkinson states the following: "We got to see a same-sex couple (or maybe even two, it's a pretty fast shot) smooching in the background at a concert scene from the show, something which constituted the Disney Channel's first same-sex kiss" (Atkinson). This is the episode "Just friends." The problem here is that it shows something that is morally questionable. This is not appropriate in children's shows because, as mentioned, children easily "absorb" what they see on TV. Children, due to their tendency to imitate, may decide to do the same thing they see.

The producers of the series focus on themes such as love, rivalry, the superhero ideal. Some episodes contain themes that are suitable for people over 16 - there is kissing, intimate relationships, violence, adult jokes. Because of all this, we must confirm that such a series should not be broadcast on a TV channel watched by younger children. The problem, however, is that liberal apologists defend similar themes present in cartoon series. It turns out that such series are "progressive" and can teach our children about "tolerance." We cannot help but think that this is done on purpose. Why is there a gay kiss in a cartoon? Who can guarantee that this trend will not continue in the future? How can we be sure that some traditional fairytales and plots will not be transformed in the context of LGBT ideology? If homosexual kisses appear today, then tomorrow we can see transgenders in animated series! And this is not a threat, it is quite likely to have happened!

Speaking of transgenders, this topic is hinted at in another series – 'Recess' (1997-2001). Overall, this series seems normal, but there are some weirder ideas shown in it: "We got a rejection of gender norms in Vince enjoying wearing high heels and TJ renaming himself Ashley" (Atkinson). Although this is a series for a more mature audience, we still ask: why do these views have to be shown in an animated film? Why the producers of such series do not make a separate series for adults only?

Surely these cases will become more frequent. In 2022, Disney has already released the full-length animated film *Lightyear*, in which a homosexual couple of two women is described. This movie provoked serious reactions not only from our conservative community, but also in Arab countries and China. We can be sure that the liberal camp will praise this movie and see only positive things. It shows how love stands above societal restrictions and stereotypes, etc. There is nothing else to expect from our liberals. But this trend is already alarming. LGBT ideology is clearly present in school, and now it is even being reinforced in movies for kids!

Someone might argue here: if we put a special rating on such shows, that would solve the problem. For example, to have a special rating for more controversial movies and shows. Parents themselves will decide what their children watch, and that is it.

But if we follow this principle, we can introduce more controversial situations into children's shows. Why not discuss issues like abortion and euthanasia? Following this principle, we can easily make a feature movie with an abortion scene. Since abortions are talked about positively in sex education classes, what is the problem with showing them in cartoons? Now we see how absurd all this is.

Children cannot decide for themselves what to watch. It is like leaving a baby to fend for himself, without supervision. We must guide our children on their journey into the world of cinema and television. There is already too much information in our media world; there are videos with controversial content everywhere. Parents and anyone caring for children should be very careful with all of this. The new media are no less dangerous because they offer an illusory picture of consumers who are on good terms with each other. And in fact, this is a world where a child can come across videos with violence, eroticism, drugs and many other inappropriate elements.

Although there is a rating system to indicate which film is suitable for young children and which is not, it is not enough. With this easy access to TV today (a child can easily turn on TV access on their phone without their parents even knowing), measures should be taken to limit the very content of TV shows, programs, videos on social networks. The rating system worked 25 years ago, when there was still no mass access to the Internet and no online social networks. At this point, it serves only as an assistant to parents, guiding them as to which movie is not suitable for their children. But the current rating system seems inadequate. It needs changes, and this should take place on federal level.

Do parents have time to monitor the content their children are watching? This is impossible today. The only option is to simply take the phone away from their child. Thus, the child will not have access to social networks and the videos spread across them. The truth is that today it is best if children under 12 do not possess smartphones. It is good for parents to be in touch with them through phones that do not have internet access. But beyond that, federal lawmakers need to step in, too. In modern TV shows, there are many segments full of violence and eroticism. They are distributed freely and without censorship. A special law should be prepared to curb these scenes.

Yes, such a bill would limit free speech. Yes, this bill will strip movie producers of their civil rights. It would also lead to a decrease in their huge profits. But it will leave the morals of our children intact.

Another example we can give in this regard is the series *Game of Thrones*. This series is full of elements of eroticism and brutal violence. At times we see quite pornographic scenes as well as terrible cruelty. So if these scenes were missing from the series, would this show have delivered its message? Yes, it certainly would. This series would be no less interesting. The cruelties shown in it are completely unnecessary. Viewers can just picture them in their imagination. The erotic scenes are completely unnecessary; they have absolutely no role to play in developing the plot. There are some controversial moments such as the incest shown in the series. We clearly see that eroticism and brutal violence have no role here. Perhaps these erotic and violent scenes made the show one of the most popular in recent decades.

Has our perception of television changed so much that we no longer react with anger to such series? Just 20 years ago, many of us would have protested against such a perversion of the notion of cinema. The producers themselves would never release such production in our movie theaters. Today, this series is even something of a benchmark, and other series follow it. For example, many people are watching 'Vikings,' in which we also see brutal violence. Tomorrow other similar series and TV shows will appear. All this must stop now because at some point our conception of the beautiful will be lost forever!

What happened to our society after the 1960s? Why have we allowed this depravity in society itself? Why did we let it into the television and the media?

The explanation is that all this happened gradually. First, they explained to us that this was part of the "freedom of the person." Then we were told that we would become "more solidary" when we eliminated discrimination in this country. But the understanding of discrimination has expanded to such an extent that it now includes even LGBT people. So it turned out that they also have the right to "protection from discrimination." Today it is already very difficult to show your attitude to LGBT ideology without fear of prosecution. No wonder there will soon be mandatory quotas for LGBT characters in TV shows, including children's movies. Any criticism of such a process will be considered "discrimination" and "intolerance."

The notion of "personal freedom" is being used in a manipulative way today. Liberals explain to us that all this is necessary to protect certain groups of people. At the same time, the liberal camp increasingly restricts the freedom of other groups of people! The balance that once existed between the two camps no longer exists. There used to be a kind of compromise that allowed both conservatives and liberals to live their lives normally, according to their views. This is not the case today because the liberal way of life is not only tolerated, but enforced as well.

Evidently, freedom of speech is a great thing; in this country everyone has the right to express their opinion about something. But let us imagine this freedom in relation to terrorists. Can we allow a group of terrorists to freely communicate with each other and plan attacks? Obviously, we cannot. Hence, in some cases this freedom is subject to limitation. And why cannot LGBT ideology be compared to terrorism? It not only corrupts young people, but also destabilizes our society. At a time when we need to seriously protect our interests in the world and our national security, we are dealing with the rights of groups of people who do not need such protection!

Research shows that Americans generally favor free speech, but not *unlimited* speech. In recent years, the manipulations we have seen on social media have made us more suspicious and critical. People's attitude toward new media has changed and now fewer people believe what is spread there. We already know that certain groups of people and organizations are behind certain fake news. Russian meddling in the 2016 election showed that it is very important that the new media is also regulated. We cannot leave them without monitoring. Therefore, we must act in the direction of putting some limitations.

A recent Pew Research Center poll addresses the question of whether big tech companies should be regulated by the government. In short, can the federal government impose restrictions on those companies (specifically, the new media), and can they control the content that their users distribute. Some situations warrant such control: for example, interference by external forces in our elections; terrorist threat, etc. The complete denial of obvious facts cannot also have origin from outside.

A slight majority of respondents claim that there should be government control: "Growing shares of Americans think major technology companies should face more government regulation, and a majority say that these firms have too much economic power and influence" (Vogels par. 1). A serious problem, according to the respondents, is the merger of the big companies (for example, Facebook, Whatsapp and Instagram). This allows them to expand their influence without the user realizing it. This increase also eliminates competition.

According to the survey, "Some 56% of Americans think major technology companies should be regulated more than they are now, and 68% believe these firms have too much power and influence in the economy." So it turns out that "The latest survey represents a statistically significant increase of those who say there should be more regulation, up from 47% in June 2020 and 51% in May 2018" (Vogels par. 2). No doubt, this percentage will increase, especially as we witness the pro-Russian and pro-China campaigns in the new media.

Another conclusion from this survey concerns whether tech companies have too much influence today: "Overall, 68% of adults say major tech companies have too much power and influence in today's economy" (Vogels par. 12). Of course, this does not mean that we must necessarily reduce this influence. But it is important to realize that this influence may be increasing, and certain groups and interests may be behind it.

In recent years, for example, Facebook has been forced to warn its users about (1) fake news or unproven claims, (2) content distributed by Russian and Chinese state media, (3) sponsored content during election campaigns. Also, Facebook is exercising stronger control over the content on its platform.

However, here we can also see a weakness in the ambition for stronger regulation. Without a doubt, Facebook heavily censors conservative groups and users and favors liberal politicians and ideology. For example, a user can be blocked just for commenting about LGBT people. What would happen if a government run by liberals used the new media to spread liberal ideology?

That is why it is necessary to specify exactly what the restricted content should be in new media, TV shows and even in music videos. When a person is given full power to censor, he usually censors opinions he does not like.

Is this battle lost? Does it make sense to fight against people like the creators of the *Lightyear* movie? Our legislation fully protects LGBT people. From this point of view, how can we ban homosexual kisses in children's movies?

All this means that we have to start from legislation. LGBT ideology should not have the character of dogma. Criticism of this ideology should not be criminalized. The legislation on discrimination needs to be revised first. This could also happen following a challenge to this legislation before the Supreme Court. Right now there is a chance for something like that to happen. It must be precisely and clearly specified that all U.S. citizens have equal rights, and no group should have more rights than other citizens.

Can the government really control the media the way we want it to? This is a difficult task. Control always starts with the family. It becomes easier when the child is in homeschooling mode. Then what the child learns can be combined with what the child watches on TV. After that comes the role of the school, and finally the institutions and federal or state agencies.

It is also important to create NGOs to support conservative families. Such NGOs must (1) provide educational services and (2) various activities for children when they are not in school. More activities for the kids means less TV. Staying at home mothers should also be legislatively supported so that they have more control over their children (instead of delegating these tasks to nannies). It is crucial to give financial incentives to mothers staying on longer maternity. For example, let mothers receive financial bonuses for the first three years after giving birth. This will help families stabilize themselves financially and meet this challenge. It is not right for young children to be left with a babysitter or go to daycare - this furthers their isolation from the family and makes them seriously dependent on the government.

Creating and supporting conservative media is also a good option, but again, it is good for children to have as little access to television as possible. Therefore, it is necessary that their free time be well organized. Thus, these children themselves will be far from watching TV for hours. This is where the role of church organizations and communities comes in - the inclusion of children should take place at an early age. This is our birthright and we should not deviate from it. Yes, the liberal camp is anxious to prohibit the introduction of religion to young children, and we need to react to this.

However, the influence of the media should not make parents feel like they have no responsibility toward their children. On the contrary, *parents are (almost) solely responsible for their children's behavior and values.* Although we live in a world of debauchery and hedonism, it does not mean that we have no role to play in this world. People create patterns of behavior; these patterns do not come out of nowhere.

We must set a personal example for our children, the children around us. We should not be engaged only with our work or our personal problems. Today, unfortunately, we work 10 hours a day, 50 hours a week. We hardly have time to be with our family. We do not have time to play with our children. Our children are left in kindergarten or at school where someone else takes care of them; someone else educates them, someone else gives them knowledge about the world. So it is very easy for an external force to promote certain ideas and get them into the heads of innocent children.

We, as parents and as a society in general, are abdicating our responsibilities to the children of this country. Civic activism and awareness of parental responsibility is the way that will lead us out of this spiritual crisis.

Certainly, legislative initiatives are also needed. Naturalistic scenes of violence as well as eroticism should be thrown out of our TV shows and video materials. It does not matter what category a movie or show is in; these scenes should not be shown at all. Of course, Hollywood is not going to be thrilled with this, but this legislative change needs to happen.

As already mentioned, from an artistic point of view, not everything that happens in a work of art needs to be shown on the screen. Let the viewers imagine these scenes of violence for themselves if they want; but these naturalistic scenes should not materialize. There are beautiful classical movies from the 1960s with little violence; it does not have to be violent or overtly erotic for a movie to be appealing. True art relies on viewers' imagination; it does not need to depict everything that takes place in this work of art. A given movie is realistic not because it shows everything in naturalistic way; it rather turns to individual problems and connects them with social problems; it connects individual with society. This is true realism- to show the unique interconnectedness of all persons in one society.

Regarding kids' TV shows, one thing is clear: they should deal with purely children's things, and not with topics such as intimate love, "gender identity," racism, etc. Love can be affected within family and friendship love. And *homosexual scenes should be completely excluded from educational materials and TV shows for kids.* These attempts must be reacted to today because tomorrow such scenes will become something normal. Therefore, there is an urgent need for a law on the content of children's media, which clearly specifies what exactly cannot be shown there (including commercials). We know that today's shows for kids need to be "educational," and this is something to praise. But there is nothing in legislation that prohibits features that could do harm to kids' mental health. How can we protect our kids from damaging influence if legislators have not thought about this?

Legislation is the proper way to change this. As we mentioned, current legislation puts too much emphasis on sexual orientation and "gender identity." Some LGBT people (or their advocates) can easily file a suit against anyone opposing same-sex kisses in TV shows for kids. By changing legislation, we should receive more legal support in such circumstances.

The media is very influential, but it is not like a monster that we cannot deal with. The unification of all conservative forces will bring about the necessary legislative changes. Obviously, the issue of eroticism and violence in television will be difficult to solve, but it is not impossible. The freedom of speech is an essential part of our society, it is the foundation of America herself. But this freedom is not absolute, it cannot exceed the safety of our society. And when America is threatened by external forces, we cannot simply state that "the freedom of speech is the basis of our Constitution." The freedom of speech is to say what you think, what is your opinion on a given issue; but it is not expressed in spreading mentally harmful images, images that actually do not reflect the reality, real life. Because real life is much more that any individual can grasp and perceive. Life is love, kindness, mutual care; it is creation, friendships, connections. All that we see on the TV is far from real; it is merely a distorted image of reality.

Conclusion

Many decades ago, children were heavily exploited. They were denied access to education. They had to work as much as mature people. Children had no rights, and rarely did anyone protect them.

But today things are different. Children have various rights - to education, to a normal life in a normal family, to health care, to activities and occupations. Almost all over the world, children have similar rights. It is the mark of a highly civilized society to safeguard these rights and ensure that children live happily and carefree.

Unfortunately, these rights are being abused a lot nowadays, putting a certain pressure on the minds of our children. It is said that children should be "tolerant of LGBT people," of transgender people, "non-binary persons" etc. It is believed that the rights of parents should be limited and that the government can raise and educate children instead of their parents. Children are taken from their families without reason; strange educational materials are introduced at school; they watch movies for kids that sometimes contain controversial moments. What is going on?

All this does not happen by accident; it is not the result of some invisible "societal changes." It is the result of purposeful actions of a certain group of people. They believe that by educating our children according to their model, future generations will already easily adopt their ideology. In short, *education is a tool in the hands of people preaching liberal ideology.*

Therefore, our call must be: return the children to their parents! Give parents maximum freedom to raise and educate their children. Allow the children themselves to choose their path, their values, their moral norms. America today does not need an official ideology to be imposed in school and by the media. We just need more freedom.

Return the children to their parents so that these children can live and grow up happily. Give this chance to our children so they can be the backbone of a future America. Save our children from the mental and physical trauma stemming from the insanity of LGBT ideology. Save them from "gender re-assignment" and all such fabrications that aim to break down our society.

Our message should be: Reduce federal and state control on the family. Make families autonomous units that can decide for themselves how to live and how to contribute to our common well-being. We have nothing against liberal families raising their children as they wish; but this model of upbringing should not be imposed on all of us, with our money.

America was founded by people seeking freedom from the regimes in Europe. Today, this freedom is severely restricted - whether with reason or not. Dominating society with an ideology that is not accepted by the majority of people is not a good idea. This must be stopped as soon as possible. If today we accept this ideology to enter our home, tomorrow our mouths will be shut by force and we will no longer have a choice, we will have no alternative.

We must take our responsibility to protect our children. This will not happen by passively watching and waiting. We must influence politicians and legislators, the judiciary and the media.

To all those who think that today there is no point in resistance and that it is very difficult to find hope, we can refer to the words once spoken by Christ: "Be always on the watch, and pray that you may be able to escape all that is about to happen, and that you may be able to stand before the Son of Man" (Luke 21:36). We must not close our eyes when we see evil, and we must not stop believing in Our Savior. These hard times will

pass and then we will know that we were stronger than we thought.

Works cited

Advocates for Youth. Myths and Facts About Comprehensive Sex Education.

https://www.advocatesforyouth.org/wp-content/uploads/storage/advfy/documents/cse-myths-and-facts.pdf

Atkinson, S. These Children's Shows Teach Some Really Huge Lessons. *Bustle*. July 19, 2019.

https://www.bustle.com/p/13-childrens-shows-that-are-actually-progressive-as-hell-70624

Barry, Ellen. In Sweden's Preschools, Boys Learn to Dance and Girls Learn to Yell. *The New York Times*, March 24, 2018.

https://www.nytimes.com/2018/03/24/world/europe/sweden-gender-neutral-preschools.html

Bartholet, Elizabeth. "Homeschooling: Parent Rights Absolutism vs. Child Rights to Education & Protection." *Arizona Law Review* vol. 62(1), 2020.

http://nrs.harvard.edu/urn-3:HUL.InstRepos:40108859

The Holy Bible. New International Version.

Curren, Randall, and Dorn, Charles. "Patriotic Education in a Global Age: A Brief Introduction." *Journal of Social Philosophy* vol. 00, 2022, pp. 1-6.

DOI: 10.1111/josp.12429

Dickerson, Adam. *John Holt. The Philosophy of Unschooling*. Springer, 2019.

European Parliament. "Comprehensive Sexuality Education: Why is It Important?" Directorate-General for Internal Policies, February 2022.

https://www.europarl.europa.eu/RegData/etudes/STUD/2022/719998/IPOL_STU(2022)719998_EN.pdf

Farenga, Patrick. "Homeschooling: Creating Alternatives to Education." *Bulletin of Science, Technology & Society* Vol. 18 (2), 1998, pp. 127-33.

Gaither, Milton. "Why Homeschooling Happened." *Educational Horizons* vol. 86 (4), 2008, pp. 226-37.

Gaudiano, Nicole. Trump Creates 1776 Commission to Promote 'Patriotic Education.' *Politico*, November 2, 2020. https://www.politico.com/news/2020/11/02/trump-1776-commission-education-433885

Huber, Valerie, and Firmin, Michael. "A History of Sex Education in the United States since 1900." *International Journal of Educational Reform* vol. 23(1), 2014, pp. 26-51.

Plato. *The Republic*. Transl. by C. D. C. Reeve. Hackett Publishing, 2004.

Reimann, Thor. Patriotic Education: Pride or Problem? *Harvard Political Review*. August 2, 2021. https://harvardpolitics.com/patriotic-education/

Mannes, Marc. "Family Preservation: A Professional Reform Movement". *The Journal of Sociology & Social Welfare* vol. 20(3) , Article 2, 1993. https://scholarworks.wmich.edu/jssw/vol20/iss3/2

NCHR (Nordic Committee for Human Rights). Report: Child Removal Cases in Sweden and the Neighbouring Nordic Countries. December 10, 2012. https://www.nkmr.org/docs/Report_to_the_Council_of_Europe_-_Child_Removal_Cases_in_Sweden_and_the_Nordic_countries.pdf

Sacred Congregation for Catholic Education. Educational Guidance in Human Love. Outlines for Sex Education, 1983.

https://www.vatican.va/roman_curia/congregations/ccatheduc/documents/rc_con_

ccatheduc_doc_19831101_sexual-education_en.html

Simonsen, Jan, and Haslev Skånland, Marianne. A Case Exposing the Double Standards

of Norway's CPS. May 12, 2018, *Sunday Guardian.live*

https://www.sundayguardianlive.com/lifestyle/case-exposing-double-standards-

norways-cps

Trivedi, Shanta. "The Harm of Child Removal." *New York University Review of Law &*

Social Change vol. 43, pp. 523-80, 2019.

https://scholarworks.law.ubalt.edu/all_fac/1085

Vogels, Emily. 56% of Americans Support More Regulation of Major Technology

Companies. Pew Research Center, July 20, 2021.

https://www.pewresearch.org/fact-tank/2021/07/20/56-of-americans-support-

more-regulation-of-major-technology-companies/

Westheimer, Joel. "Politics and Patriotism in Education." *Phi Delta Kappan* April 2006,

pp. 608-20.

Whewell, Tim. Norway's Barnevernet: They Took our Four Children… Then the Baby.

BBC, April 14, 2016. https://www.bbc.com/news/magazine-36026458

WHO Regional Office for Europe and BZgA. Standards for Sexuality Education in

Europe. A Framework for Policy Makers, Educational and Health Authorities and

Specialists, 2010.

https://www.bzga-whocc.de/fileadmin/user_upload/BZgA_Standards_English.pdf

Zeiler, Alean. "Abstinence Education." *The Linacre Quarterly* vol. 81 (4) 2014, 372–7.